Not Counted

No, I Matter I Have a Voice!!!

And The Creation of the Four Amp Resolve

Not Counted

No, I Matter I Have a Voice!!!

And The Creation of the Four Amp Resolve

An individual call to action for the unemployed/underemployed/ employment threatened who are not counted in the labor participation rate.

Patrick M. Palella

Edited by Maria Cesar

authorHOUSE®

AuthorHouse™
1663 Liberty Drive
Bloomington, IN 47403
www.authorhouse.com
Phone: 1-800-839-8640

Published by AuthorHouse 10/15/2013

ISBN: 978-1-4918-2918-9 (sc)
ISBN: 978-1-4918-2917-2 (e)

Library of Congress Control Number: pending

To my father—a smart, kind man who was not counted for thirty plus years.

To my mother—The hardest working woman I have ever known, thanks mom.

Preface

As I write this book our nation is celebrating the reduction of the unemployment rate to 7.4% while stock market traders are fretting over the "tapering" by the Federal Reserve. Several articles are circulating claiming the real unemployment rate is 11.3% or even higher. The labor participation rate is at a thirty year low despite the growing population. I watch the talking heads on the financial networks and I smile because it is difficult to celebrate the creation of the increase in the number of part-time jobs. When I listen to these employment statistics I think of my discussions with three "consultants." What do you call an unemployed executive? A consultant! Recently I had lunch with one consultant who presented me with a strong portfolio of quality work. By the end of the meeting he confided to me that he needed to sell personal assets to survive. Personal asset is a broad term. He was not talking about stocks and bonds; he meant jewelry, heirlooms and items of sentimental significance.

Thirty years ago we came out of school filled with hope and the energy to make our marks on the world in the same way our parents' generation did. Some of us succeeded within one organization for the whole of our career. Others moved along the corporate land-scape by changing employers. Either way we were contributors who had endless opportu-nities. We rode the coat tails of Reagonimics and we helped our nation regain the global prominence that we lost in the seventies. We enjoyed our prosperity but many of us were constantly tempted by the next opportunity. Our energy was high and our self-esteem was even higher. Then the music stopped and many of us were without a chair. We thought it was temporary and the band would play again but for many it did not. The hope and prosperity that had consumed us had been replaced with the challenges of erratic reve-nue streams, aging parents, escalating higher education costs and the looming weight of our own retirement.

I am not an academic, psychologist or self-help guru. I am a typical long-term unem-ployed senior executive; father, brother, friend and American. My educational back ground is somewhat of an enigma. I have an MBA from a top 25 program yet I never finished a Bachelors degree. I was one of the youngest Vice Presidents of a major Wall Street firm who in the middle of that career decided to go back to school to study management. Since earning my MBA I have been the President of two successful turn-around situations one of which was owned by one of Wall Street's most prestigious LBO/Private Equity firms. In spite of my education and experience, for the past seven years I have endured sporadic employment and I have had to take a mercenary approach to my mental and fiscal survival. During this period I kept my sons in private schools and I did not alter any aspect of their lives. This book is about more than making money. It is about how the cloistered existence and the lack of human interaction can destroy a person. This book is not only about financial survival. It is about how this professional purgatory negatively affects the mind, the body and the soul. In this book we will explore how to shatter the hidden shackles of the contemporary business environment. If you read this book I hope you find one idea that helps you. If not at least you will know that you are not alone and you count.

Contents

CHAPTER 1

An Erie Silence

*"Nothing splendid has ever been
achieved except by those who dared
believe that something inside them
was superior to circumstance."*
Bruce Barton

It is 7 a.m. on a gray rainy Monday morning. The thud of the garage door closing tells me my spouse is off to work. Her salary is our life line for the basics of food, mortgage and health insurance. My boys ask me for a twenty dollar bill to go to the hockey rink. I give it to them with a smile on my face and a gnawing pit in my stomach. They leave and I tune into CNBC to hear the current news. Featured on the program could be an interview with a former contemporary or past subordinate of mine who now enjoys national prominence in the business world. Since there is nothing on my daily agenda, I have not yet shaved or showered. I turn down the volume on the television swearing a little as I boot up my best friend and co-worker the computer. I sit in near silence; the rain tapping on the window is my only company. It is now 7:45 a.m. and like clockwork my neighbor backs his car out of the garage on his way to his office. I know its Monday by the tie he wears. What a boring twit. Looking further out the window I see more neighbors waiting under umbrellas for busses to transport them to their downtown offices, where once I had an office. It's time to take a shower. There is no need to shave this morning because today I have no person to person meetings on my agenda. The rain continues to beat like the hangman's drum and I feel like a condemned man walking to the gallows.

With my hygienically important events behind me I try to face my list of ten important tasks at my desk. It has been my longtime habit to set up my day's agenda with a list of the ten most important tasks the night before each working day. This practice was a huge help when my daily tasks outnumbered the hours in a day. Then I check my calendar and again it is empty. Unfortunately next to the calendar is an ever growing stack of bills. The first of the month seems to roll around faster and faster each month. In an attempt to get positively focused I put the bills in a drawer. I attack my list but after the third no answer or voicemail I become anxious and frustrated. Frenetically I decide to make a new plan then I stare at a blank legal pad.

Another morning is gone. Two of my fellow unemployed brothers who want to develop a consulting firm give me a call. The discussions are always misdirected and convoluted and never proceed to an action item. Inwardly I realize that this every other day exercise is a mutual mental masturbation session. As they talk I envision three coal miners trapped in a coal mine gasping for air. I say very little and I mentally participate sparingly. While on the conference my caller identification tells me that three bill collectors are calling. Panicky I check the due dates of the utility bills. The good news is that the day is almost half over. My spouse sends me a text at lunchtime asking "How is it going?" and telling me to "Hang in there." While I appreciate the sentiment my feeling of inadequacy swells. Another day is getting past me. I want nothing more than one positive event to boost my spirits. I keep reminding myself to stay focused and to think. Then I return to the plan I made last night. And I try to forge ahead but to no avail.

As I make more calls the afternoon slowly passes. I think about a few business strategies and another day draws to a close. My spouse arrives home and I ask her about her day. She then proceeds to tell me about the events and happenings of the people and the projects in her department. I am ashamed to say that I cringe with envy because she has a community and sense of purpose and belonging even though she may have had a daunting day. When we sit down to dinner I listen to the boys talk about their college plans which makes the hair on my neck stand up. Next I can hear the fluids gurgle in my stomach. Even though I try to smile and I try to be encouraging the feelings of intense inadequacy and failure return. As the meal passes I feel compelled to over compensate. So I clean up the kitchen while hoping to convey a sense of calm and a sense direction for my ship. This ship which is sinking is my family. The kids ask to use the car to go visit their cousin who lives twenty miles away. My first thought is the cost of the gas. But of course I tell them to go and to be careful.

It is time for my evening exercise of writing out my ten most important task list for the next day. With a legal pad and pen in hand I push my brain for new productive ideas. I consider another all-out resume blitz. Then I think about the eight hundred or so resumes and carefully crafted cover letters that I already submitted and the sparse responses to those efforts. I could kick myself for posting my resume on so many useless job boards and I am even angrier about throwing out good money for some of these job boards. I get tired thinking about all the networking breakfasts where my expectations rose because I heard a friend promise that he/she would speak to someone on my behalf. The compounded disappointments resulting from these meetings have only served to deepen my sense of inadequacy. These constant rejections are pounding me into the ground. I want to drop on my knees and ask God what I have done to be caught in this rubrics cube of razor blades. My perception of who I am now, compared to who I was, has been gradually chipping away at my confidence. A heavy shroud of total inadequacy seems to cover me. My mind is full of destructive thoughts. Fear, anger, jealousy and hopelessness are raging through me. I look around and I see that nothing has changed or has grown except the inches on my waist line, the number of cigarette butts in the ashtray and the stack of bills in my desk.

I did not realize what was happening to me because the changes were so gradual. Unfortunately they have proven to be significant. These changes manifested themselves in ways I did could not have imagined. My voice has lost its crispness and its authoritative nature which makes me sound weak and timid. When communicating with someone I always feel lost because he/she has an agenda and I do not. My body is sedentary and the results of that condition are compounding. My demeanor is one of underlying sadness. I am not aware of all that has changed and I continue to retreat but I think I am being proactive. Those close to me can see the damage but are hesitant to confront me. Often they see me drift mentally miles away and I am sure they wonder where I have gone. I watch the television news until one thirty in the morning feeling as if life for me has become a spectator sport. I am a shell of my former self. If I do not wake up from this self-induced trance soon it is going be too late. Not only am I lost in my own home, but in my own mind, in my own body and in my own soul. Now I am no more than a shell of my former self. The things and the events that in the past brought me joy in the past, especially my son's sporting events now seem like intrusions on my miserable comfort of malaise. I walk around with a scowl on my face making even strangers think I am upset with them. I continue to go through the motions but I am starting to realize that I threw in the towel some time ago.

Getting back to the events of my Monday evening I feel fortunate that something as minute as a run to the grocery store gives me relief from my sanctuary of despair. So I eagerly run the errand. It is about seven thirty in the evening and I realize that this is the first time I have set foot outdoors all day. As I walk down the aisles of the store looking at the name brands and corporate logos I ask myself: Can't anyone use my talents? In the checkout line I watch the young man bagging groceries and I realize that he is earning more money today than me. It is unbelievable that I am envious of a high school student who bags groceries for minimum wage. Then I notice a man in a suit also waiting in line. He seems pensive with a sense of urgency causing him to be in a hurry. My convoluted perception is that he has somewhere to go but I can stand in this line all night. I am afraid my emotional reaction to my convoluted perception is apparent in the way I exit the store. As eager as I was to leave my sanctuary of despair now I can't wait to get back in the car and get back to the four walls that I have come to detest.

The next day is a repeat of the previous day with the exception of a lunch appointment with an old business acquaintance. Oh boy I get to put a suit on. I try to prepare myself by guarding against unjustified optimism. As I drive through the busy downtown financial district I reminisce about my successful days in this area of the city. I feel cheated and left out akin to being the only kid in the class not invited to a classmate's party. I look up and see a building that houses an office that I occupied fifteen years ago. Suddenly I wonder where the time has gone. My negative thought processes shift into high gear taking a path of its own and I begin to second guess every decision I have ever made. Yet another mental battle ensues minutes before the time of the meeting. This mental battle causes a startling realization. I realized that in the past I was prepared and focused for important meetings. Not surprisingly when I get to my destination I feel bit queasy. So I put up a stiff upper lip and proceed. We get through the small talk and I swallow the braggadocios description of my associates new summer home and his son's football scholarship. Then he hits me up. From me he wants an introduction to one of my former colleagues. Ironically I have had trepidation about calling this colleague on my own behalf. Not once has my lunch companion expressed any interest in me or what I am doing. Due to his superficial nature, he probably assumes that all is well because I am dressed professionally. Riding on his assumption I allow my pride to block another opportunity. The lunch winds down and I have said nothing and asked for nothing. The only redeeming factor of this meeting would be for him to pick up the check.

Once we part company I walk through my city club which has been my refuge for over three decades. Suddenly I feel like a stranger. I try to ignore memories of more dynamic and successful times. Friends who notice me ask where I have been and even the clubs employees remark about my scarce attendance. I viewed this place, in the not so distance past as my second home, I now feel awkward and out of place. Since I have time to kill I force myself to stay at the club in the event I run into an old acquaintance that possibly could steer me in direction of some work or consulting opportunities. It is disgusting to realize that I have reduced my career strategy to the hope of a chance meeting. In a building that has always been my retreat and sanctuary I almost feel like a degenerate loitering in a bus station.

As the afternoon looms ahead of me I am stuck in the financial district. Seeing that I already have a thirty dollar parking fee charge I decide to try to make the trip worthwhile. So I call some former colleagues. They suggest I stay around for an early cocktail. The two people I meet for drinks are close acquaintances both of whom work at the nation's largest bank. I met them several years earlier at a vendor's Christmas function. Neither person is in senior management but they have great work ethics. The evening begins with the usual small talk and then the discussion shifts to the economy. They have concerns about the new Dodd/Frank legislation and what that legislation could do to their industry. Another major concern is the effect of the Dodd/Frank legislation on their company's stock price. In the past few years both of these individuals have earned multiple promotions. At one time

I held a position of their boss's, bosses' boss. They make in a year what I used to make in a month and just as I felt envious of the grocery store bag boy I now feel envious of these two friends. During our conversation they discussed the responsibilities of their most recent positions. Thinking back to my early career days I remember how great it felt to be recognized as a critical part of the organization and I try to be happy for my companions. It's time for the evening to wind down. They stick me with the bar tab because in their minds I am extremely wealthy. Envy and inner embarrassment consume me and it's time for my long fruitless day to come to an end so I head back home.

The next morning starts like the previous two mornings. I get my cup of coffee from the tin I purchased at Costco and think back to the barista at Starbucks who always had my coffee waiting because she thought I was a busy person with important things to do. The news day is heavy with politics and sports. I miss the opportunities for discussions at the water cooler and there is no with whom to exchange points of view or even a joke. Without realizing it I talk to the news anchor as if he could hear me. After formulating my individual opinions about the day's news, I return to my solitary business in silence. My life is now the antithesis of what it was before I joined the ranks of the unemployed/underemployed/employment threatened.

Today I am a consultant. Tomorrow I might submit resumes for available positions. There is absolutely no plan or consistency in my actions. Today is a very proactive day because I try to make rain by calling several associates and friends. I unearth a few possibilities but the possibilities are out in the future. Nonetheless in the end it is good day because I acted proactively and know of some long term prospects. But somewhere deep down inside I know this is not enough.

On that very night I feel a small positive force beginning to emerge from my darkness. Then I remember a looming family function. No one outside my immediate family is aware of the severity of my situation. So tonight I need to turn in a stellar performance. My spouse is uncomfortable and forces a smile as she listens to trivial complaints from the rest of the family. The evening finally ends. With their excellent performances behind them every member of my nuclear family should be nominated for an academy award. The ride home is quiet.

I realize that sometimes perceptions are not reality. As I stated earlier no one outside our nuclear family knows of our situation however based on tonight's gathering it seems other factions of the family are doing quite well. The issue is that when others seem to be living their lives with no fiscal, professional or emotional disruption you feel as if a chasm is widening in your life that may never be filled. I decide enough austerity and pick up a dozen dough-nuts for the boys.

Well it is Thursday and the good news is we are in the final stretch of the week. I feel like an emotional speed bag. My two wounded con-sulting brothers try to call me and talk about the phantom consulting firm. I ignore the call. Instead I decide to focus on industries where I have experience. This exercise turns out to be another dead end and because this is the end of the week I tell myself to wrap it up un-til next Monday. Once again I organize my desk by putting bills in due date order; I play solitaire and look at the upcoming television schedule. Convincing myself that I need to do something productive I decide to once again scroll through the job boards and read my spam emails that tell me if I use ABC resume service I will get the perfect job within sixty days. Twice I have made the mistake of believing false claims of resume services. (Ouch that is embarrassing). My decision to be productive really was just a waste of time. The realization that another week has ended with no revenue, no quality job prospect or no viable short term consulting opportunity haunts me. My self-concept is lower now than it was on the past rainy Monday morning. I begin to doubt if I will ever see the following words of reassurance: Pay to the order of me. I wonder if I will ever have a "first" day on a new job and I imagine who my new boss might be. Friday arrives and my first thought is of the lost month of revenue that cannot be recaptured (Realizing that I was a higher level executive who is undergoing long term unemployment and I am over forty). So I panic. My week ends and I know in the recesses of my soul that I am no better off than I was five days ago. The clock tells me it is four thirty p.m. and as a result of my destructive thought process I remember past Fridays when I celebrated yet another triumphant work week with my team. Now I hitch up my sweat pants and head to the kitchen. The weekend ahead promises nothing but a different brand of isolation and despair. Now you get the picture.

The previous narrative described one typical week in the past several years of my life. And I still could have been spinning in that downward spiral. I realize the preceding pages make *Death of a Salesman* look like a light cheerful read. One might think I was clinically depressed. And at times I am sure I was. I know that during that period I wallowed in self-pity and self-absorption. So much so that I was willing to take jobs at considerably less compensation. But even lower paying opportunities were not offered to me. Just to feel productive I was willing to work for a third of my prior income. Compounding the problem for those of us unemployed/underemployed/ employment threatened individuals is the realization that recent college graduates, also willing to work for far less money, are not finding positions. These are unprecedented times in our nation's history. A jobless economic recovery, technology that increases the hourly production per employee both have contributed to a reduced workforce. The employment terrain has changed completely during the course of our careers. (Yes, some of us remember the "pink" message pad). There are hundreds of career sites on the internet but it is difficult to decipher those that are legitimate from those that are scams. To sum it up we are working within an employment terrain that is constantly changing.

I knew I was approaching rock bottom one Saturday morning when I visited one of my dearest friends. He too has been facing many economic and emotional challenges. We have an open and honest relationship so we can speak freely to each other. He owns a private security firm so he legally carries a fire arm. He comes from a wealthy background and in the past he sought my advice and council regarding family business decisions. His problems are not of a financial nature. But because he is a trusting person people always take serious advantage of him. Greater than the financial loss is his loss of faith and confidence in his fellow man. He sold his family's company seven years ago so like me he is trying regain his employment direction. During our visit he was getting dressed for work so his pistol was on his bed. I never owned a fire arm and I only fired one once at a firing range. Staring at the gun I asked my friend to get the gun out of my site. Then I dropped to my knees in tears and said I can't take it anymore. His reaction was shock and concern. He wanted to know the root of my depression and then he took the time to give me the perspective

I needed. Before I left he gave me five one hundred dollar bills to give to the boys. Then he said you have two great sons which was his way of telling me I have so much to live for. We talked for an hour or so and I headed home shaken by the events of that visit.

Brothers and sisters we are here, this is it. If you have been out of the workforce for over eighteen months and you are over the age of forty five, your chances of returning to the employment world of the past are slim to none. Your future lies in your ability to be self-motivated so you can create long and short term income opportunities. The malaise and darkness of the first few pages is not the mission of this manuscript. Those pages serve as a point of reference from which we will learn to master by learning how to change direction. This book does not contain the magical resume or the knock their socks off cover letter. It also does not contain the five magical secrets to starting a successful consulting firm. It is not filled with academic psychological terms from someone with the security of academic tenure. This book is about how a common man, struggling in our unemployed/underemployed/employment threatened environment, grabbed himself by the ankles and lifted himself out of a desperate situation to one of positive actions and results. In other words I now control my own destiny. My control is driven by resources that have been in my mind, in my body and in my soul for my entire life. This is not a George Baily moment ("It's a Wonderful Life") where all his friends gathered to pass the hat while George reached in his waist jacket pocket to find Zuzu's pedals. This book is about facing realities, demons and the cold hard facts of the contemporary employment landscape. It is about discipline, sacrifice, deep tenacity, acceptance of where you are, letting go of where you have been and finally what you need do to get where you want to be.

We are all emotionally wired in different ways. Some of us are visual while others respond by auditory stimuli. We can be and sometimes need to be emotionally charged. Take the time to find out how you are wired. This is critical. By emotionally charged I don't mean getting "pumped" as you would when your hockey team comes on to the ice to a heavy metal medley. What I do mean is analyzing the senses to learn the emotional drive and the internal response to that drive which will uncover a true sense of self. Jarring one's senses out of engrained responses allows the

It was later in the afternoon of the Saturday afternoon that my meltdown occurred and I was on my deck which overlooks the Chicago River. I was into my usual pace, fret and smoke regime that had become my way of life. I was on the deck so much that month that I swear the neighbors thought I was the neighborhood watch commander. I had just melted down in front of a good friend which was totally out of character. I was freaked out by what happened to me a few hours earlier. The depth of the situation was like nothing I have ever felt and it was almost an out of body experience. I wanted to block out all noise so I put in my iPod ear buds. At first I did not realize that I was listening to the music from the Ron Howard's movie "Apollo Thirteen" in which the musical score was composed by James Horner. It just so happens that "Apollo Thirteen" is one of my favorite films. Suddenly my emotions went from a negative low to a positive high. I found myself feeling every movement of the score. I remembered the launch scene were the faces of three astronauts looked distorted because their flesh appeared to be compressed by the G forces. The soon to be crippled space craft had already been propelled through the atmosphere. I had not seen the movie in three years yet it played vividly in my head just as if I had watched it the night before. I still did not understand what was so moving about this music. So I thought about the film and I said to myself, Four Amps.

The essence of the story of "Apollo Thirteen" is that the United States had a crippled space craft that caused a mission to the moon to be aborted. This presented the challenge of returning the space craft and its three astronauts safely home. The crippled craft was equipped with many advanced electrical components necessary to reenter earth's atmosphere. Mission control made the decision to power down the craft to conserve vital resources. Once the ship was powered down they realized they were short Four Amps needed to repower the crippled craft with what was needed for a successful reentry. Before the launch the crew had to make a last minute adjustment. Ken Mattingly, a key member of the crew was grounded due to the possibility of a contagious medical condition. Mattingly became essential to the reentry plan of the crippled craft. He assumed this arduous task under brutal time constraints with the lives of three of his fellow moon pilots at risk. Because he was an astronaut we know three things about Mattingly. He was physically fit; he was intelligent and he was trained to make quick decisions under pressure. His challenge was to create the reentry sequence and calculate the resources needed to return the crippled craft to earth. Mattingly and his team had to design make shift apparatuses only using materials they knew to be on the space craft. Their task needed to be completed in a short number of hours or three men would orbit the earth for eternity. Adding to his stress and pressure mission control constantly asked Mattingly for progress updates. Under incredible pressure Mattingly performed brilliantly. He found the Four Amps. The three astronauts returned safely in the crippled craft. As I thought about Mattingly's heroic feat of composure and determined performance it hit me. What if I lived everyday as if I had to find Four Amps?

I wrestled for hours with that question and began to realize several critical flaws in my approach to navigating through this new career landscape. It was controlling me; I was not controlling it. I had lost all confidence, perspective and most of all faith in myself and my fellow man. Then I started to create my own reentry check list. At first it seemed daunting and useless but I knew I had to fight the demon of defeat. The list has one area that has to be reconciled before the key elements could be addressed. This is the fiscal inventory or approach that I will cover in chapter two. The real elements I realized I had to retool were my mind, my body and my soul. Sounds like a cliché but each element contributes equally to one's success or one's failure. I viewed myself as if I were a company that needed to produce Four Amps so I had to review and analyze each division of this company. I am a manager after all that should have been obvious! Not to overwhelm myself I broke down the components and I vowed to myself to look at each individual component. Often we feel overloaded because we only look at the total picture. I did as my ancestors the Romans did, divide and conquer. I went on the attack and started finding my path to Four Amps.

CHAPTER 2

Fiscal Realities

"Don't be disquieted in time of adversity. Be firm with dignity and self-reliant vigor."

Chiang Kai-Shek

We have all heard the saying, "expenses rise to meet incomes." This sounds silly when the salary keeps increasing and the bonuses and stock options are flooding in. You keep improving your life style with the quality of the goods and services you purchase. When the perks stop you realize that there is truth in that little ditty mentioned above. When the unemployment benefits run out and the savings have been depleted the electric bill still comes and the kids don't lose their appetites. The thing we call life continues even when our paychecks stop. How do I manage this situation and reengineer my finances without totally destroying my family's lifestyle? This is the point when I became my own chief financial officer (CFO). When money flowed freely often purchases and decisions were made without the same scrutiny one might find in a purchasing department that has to answer to the CFO, who has to answer to board of directors. Even if past practices had been well thought out the present realization is that money needs to be found and out-going cash-flow needs to be reduced. Changing habits is difficult just as we have observed in the country of Greece. But unfortunately many of us do not have the country of Germany to bail us out. Nobody likes the term austerity. It usually provokes squeamishness from red blooded capitalists. Many people prefer the term the law of substitution. As an example I will use my switch to drinking Costco canned coffee from my daily stop at Starbucks. This is not austerity any economist knows that it is the law of substitution. It is austerity and sacrifice, to me. But more important is my goal as the CFO is to try and maintain what is important for my family.

A big fear for those facing major changes caused by financial setbacks is the effect it could have on the family especially the children. We try to maintain that part of the lifestyle that has been important to them. That does not to say that Suzy who likes the jeans from Niemen Marcus can break out in a rash if mom takes her to Old Navy. What I am saying is that Suzy has studied dance for ten years and the dance has become a significant part of her life. So try to maintain the dance lessons. Keep as many of the gory details of your situation from your children. Young children, even as young as three years old, perceive stress and tension. Unfortunately I know this to be true from firsthand experience. Believe me the effects of a past situation stayed with me a long time. Teenagers and college kids are not dumb. They know that dad wearing pajamas in the daytime is not a good signal. Maintain your dignity in front of your children. For the better part of their lives you have been their knight in the Hickey Freeman suit who went out to conquer the world for them. Try to not let them stress unless you have exhausted all means and need to make a significant change in their lives like school choices. Cut your significant other some slack. Many of them have had to rejoin the work force and they did it willingly to help ease the financial burden. Put the ego aside and try to help with maintaining the household. Your help will speak volumes. You may need to learn how to use the washer and dryer because you pull this wagon as a team. Possibly this may not be a temporary situation. (Yes I said it may not and you thought this was a self-help book.) Keep a perspective on the value of money versus the value of your relationships you hold dearest. If your family comes apart the next stop may be a cardboard box under a viaduct. Your family is the most important part of your life. You can live in a smaller house, you can drive a domestic car and you can drink Costco coffee but you cannot replace being mom or dad.

I know we just discussed protecting the children which is important. But this is also a great moment to teach your children. I do not mean sitting the kids down to explain the difference between term and whole life insurance. What I do mean is setting the right example. Demonstrating grace under pressure and sharing with them the understanding that life is not about materialism. Use this time to explore the concepts of self-reliance and how to follow one's true compass which is honesty and integrity. Teach them never to doubt their capabilities and to be thankful for the opportunities in this great country because we are free to follow our own paths. At the risk of re-peating myself, your family is the most impor-tant part of your life and that includes you. It is important to take care of yourself. Find your inner peace and understand how you func-tion in other words how you are wired. These efforts should bring you closer together as a family because you have one new perk which is time. You now have the luxury of time to dis-cuss what your child reads for school in more depth than when you were preparing an end of the quarter board presentation. You now have time to have a catch with your child in-stead of catching a flight for the purpose of calming an upset client. All this may sound utopian but it is a benefit greater than any past benefit. About twenty years ago I made a career change to executive education. I could not wait to inhabit my office in the col-lege of business. I was amazed to learn that I would be telecommuting. I was livid. My boss at that time was one the most influential peo-ple in my life. I tried every excuse in an at-tempt to convince him to reverse his decision. Since my twin boys were four years old and I thought that my home was no environment for an academic executive. Three years later I made the move to director of the university's media Company. One day my former boss monthly premiums. Review your automobile policy. If you have an older vehicle such as a second or third car and if your state allows, drop the collision coverage so you only pay for liability coverage. For newer cars find out how increasing the deductible can reduce the premium. You might also want to look at the limits on the medical claim payment amounts of your policy. Making these adjustments can reduce your premiums significantly saving you a substantial amount of money. Now you are probably thinking I am a risk junky but nothing could be further from the truth. The harsh reality is as far as you being the target of a law suit go; you probably do not have as much to lose as you did several years ago. Sorry but that's the truth. The greater risk is no insurance coverage. So it makes sense to lower monthly insurance expenses to remain insured longer. If health insurance is not offered at your spouse's place of employment he or she may need to change employers. Health insurance is vital to your family's survival and private health insurance is prohibitively expensive. Question the necessity of owning a liability umbrella policy. If you decide you no longer need this coverage save the money. I know this paragraph won't lend me endorsements from the insurance industry, but making adjustments to my insurance policies reduce my monthly cash out lay by well over a thousand dollars. However I still feel adequately protected. Not to be redundant but this is an exercise of making your resources last as long as it possible.

Earlier I talked about the law of substitution regarding my coffee consumption. Unfortunately, if this financially challenged period is prolonged it may necessitate new forms of discipline. I need to be keenly aware of what I spend. This is part of my new job description as family CFO. Not to say that when I was a full time executive I was extravagant but never has it been never more crucial to evaluate the deployment of every dollar. This means we comparative shop at the grocery store, at the dry cleaners and for oil changes. Wednesday is double coupon day at our local grocer. You might want to find out what day it is double coupon day at your grocer. What we save is part of our total compensation. We must always keep in mind that reinventing our spending habits is vital to our survival. Believe it or not we will take great pride in our ability to maintain our family with reduced resources.

Another critical area that requires consideration is the children's schooling. At the college level financial aid is available. It is worth the time to research grants, scholarships and loans. I do not need to spend too much time on the discussion of financial aid for higher education because there are many books available on the topic. Try to find a used copy of one of these books at used book store. And do not forget about the resources on the internet. Private education through high school is the most difficult to fund. You made the decision to send your children the toniest of country day schools. The youngest child has two remaining years. Including the time of your oldest child's attendance, for the past nine years you have supported the development drives and the tuition was always paid on time. This is the point where your pride and ego conflict with your financial reality. Fortunately or unfortunately you do not lose the perception of success. Based on appearance the outside world would never think there is a necessity for you to make financial adjustments. So you make an appointment to see the head master of the country day school. You traveled to Africa six years ago on a missionary expedition with this person. You go to the meeting dressed in a Hickey Freeman suit and a Hermes tie. You park your four year old BMW in the school parking lot. Of course the headmaster does not know the suit and tie that you are the captain of the family ship so you force yourself to focus on the goal of this meeting. After the small talk you look at the headmaster and get down to business. First you sincerely express your satisfaction with his school. Now comes the difficult part. Looking him square in the eye you give him the hard facts of your family's present situation. You already know that some students receive financial assistance from the school in the form of scholarship. The goal of this meeting is to garner one of those scholarships for your daughter to avoid disrupting her academic and social progress. The volunteer development work did for the school was never meant to become a quid pro quo. But you have made an investment in the school. Now you need the school to invest in your child. In the vernacular of LaSalle Street in Chicago where I grew up I am articulately saying "hey buddy I have been good to you now I am cashing in my chip, got it?" You realize at this point your relationship with the headmaster has been altered for good. You and your family have moved from asset side of the ledger to the liability side. If he is a standup guy he tries to preserve your dignity and sympathizes with your situation. If that's the case he immediately proceeds to start the scholarship so that the critical functions of the mind, the body and the soul can operate efficiently; 2) to keep your family afloat until something really solid comes along. I know you can watch Suze on CNBC and get similar advice. But my message goes beyond the fiscal exercises. What I am proposing is that you also examine how you are wired so you can be a productive person who attacks every day with the focus of your Four Amps.

There is a potentially fun experiment that might be enabling you to generate a little cash for your cause. If you have a hobby or a skill set that you use for relaxation maybe you can profit from it. Say you have a passion to purchase vintage watches off of eBay and maybe you enjoy restoring them. Research an outlet for resale of these watches to earn a little cash from your hobby. If you make jam or bake well take a batch of your confections to the farmer's market. These activities should not become a substitute for your serious pursuit of employment or a significant consulting assignment. Let your hobby remain a hobby only let it be a cash generating hobby. If you're revenue generating hobby becomes successful enough to support your family, way to go.

I realize that reevaluation of your cash monthly outlay probably is not difficult for many readers to figure out. The challenge lies in certain areas of the process and how we approach them. We have had a visit to the headmaster at school but most likely there are more uncomfortable situations to be assessed. Take the example of a country club membership. Nobody wants to surrender dues paid five years ago. It is worth looking into whether or not the country club has a leave of absence or forbearance program. Another aspect to consider is membership of a city club. If the dues are not too steep, it might be worth holding on to membership for business reasons. Use the membership sparingly like on those occasions when courting potential consulting clients. One of the luxuries the family has always enjoyed is good food. So over the years a strong relationship with the local fish monger has developed. He calls all excited because soft shell crabs are in season and he has your standard order ready for pick up. Politely you thank him for his prompt consideration. Then you swallow your pride and tell him that you are taking a pass this year. The rewards of these tasks far outweigh the difficulty because the family ship stays its course.

So up until now we have been discussing ways to prune the bush so it grows back stronger. However there is another very important area we need to address. That is your spouse or significant other. This person is your partner sharing the emotional and fiscal burdens of the family. We the unemployed/underemployed/employment threatened can get so caught up in our challenges that we are blinded to the difficulties our partner faces on a daily basis. While performing a job he/she is forced to keep a dignified persona and positive outlook amongst his/her coworkers for at least forty hours a week. You are more than likely envious of your spouse's position and you would prefer the situation be reversed. He/she understands. Don't let this become an issue. Remember there are enough problems at home. Those problems get in the car with him/her every morning but he/she needs to keep them under wraps until he/she comes home at night. Here is a suggestion. If there is some activity that this person finds relaxing then keep it. If that means once a month your wife goes to the hair dresser at the cost of two hundred dollars so be it. She needs a brief respite from the pressures at home and the pressures of her career. If your partner is the primary bread winner and loves to golf but you are no longer members of the country club, make sure he/she gets to the driving range several times a month. Your partner may fight you but it is important to the health of his/her psyche as well as to the psyches of those around him/her. Remember he/she is keeping the roof over everyone's head, the health insurance coverage in force not to mention providing the bare necessities of life. The costs of providing some relaxation for your partner is money well spent.

Another issue worth discussing is the awareness of managing expectations both positive and negative. It is not wise to tell the family about every job interview or possible consulting opportunity. We understand the process but our children do not. Dealing with disappointment is our department not theirs. In closing I want to reiterate the following: 1) Try to keep as much of the tension and worry away from your children; 2) Your significant other is your partner in this endeavor, so always be totally honest with him/her; 3) and for fifteen minutes a day try to remove yourself from only looking at your situation and put yourself in their shoes. This practice is important because it reminds you that you live in a communal environment you call family.

what time has done to our waist and hair lines but have no concept of what the years may have done to our minds. We have all heard from either a teacher or parent this phrase "in one ear and out the other." If only that statement were true. We often do not realize at the time of an event that something either good or bad has just been filed in aisle five of our craniums. We get so caught up in the day to day challenges of life that along the way we never took time to reconcile the big ledger on our shoulders. I bet you have a regular maintenance schedule to clean and organize the files on your computer. If you neglect this task you know the end result, the machine gets slow and unresponsive. I have developed a new challenge for myself which is I ask myself often why I think a certain way. Why do I anticipate a negative outcome before it even happens? I now question the origins of my thought process and I try to consider a different outcome. Then I came to a sad realization. I loved my late father and he was a brilliant man. Unfortunately I carry many negative beliefs because of the negative outlook he passed on to me. We have all heard the term "unconditional love" which is normally associated with family relationships such as mother to son, grandparent to grandchild, and father to daughter. Often from those re-lationships our thought processes are condi-tioned with beliefs passed down from gen-eration to generation. I refer to this as an un-conditional belief. Unconditional beliefs can be good or bad. If your last name is Einstein it might even be a bonus. However most of us don't have a world changing genius in our family trees. That being the case for most of us we are probably transferring flawed beliefs from the previous generation into the minds of the next generation. Unconditional beliefs usually represent a narrow scope from certain ethnic points of view. These beliefs are harm-ful because they are based on stereo types and possibly limited exposure. We need to challenge the unconditioned beliefs which are sometimes the foundation of our deci-sion making processes. (Sorry Dad but Notre Dame is not the only university to graduate their athletes.) No disrespect to my dad or his intellect. But sometimes we must challenge lifelong unconditioned beliefs and assump-tions in order develop our own decision mak-ing processes.

I created an exercise that proved to be very interesting. I took inventory of the peo-ple who have had the most influence on my professional life. No, I didn't chase them with a bar code scanner but I relied on my memory and used the old T account methodology. I wrote down whatever I could remember about each manager. I notated physical habits, marital status, political affiliations, religious beliefs, operational methodologies, discipline styles, favorite drinks, reward structures, cars, average hours worked in a day and so on. Patterns started to evolve. I analyzed which patterns elicited responses both positive and negative. The results surprised me. If you are mathematically inclined you can assign values to certain traits and calculate a purely quantifiable exercise. The managers who seemed most like me did not reach me as well as those managers with whom I differed. I challenged the latter group of managers. This exercise enabled me to recall their most prominent and visible managerial beliefs. I compiled a list of their managerial beliefs and I started to realize where certain elements of my decision making and thought processes originated. In many ways it was both humorous and shocking. I realized the origins of my mental dichotomy. Why sometimes I totally missed the boat and why at other times my insights felt incredibly sharp. Completing this experiment took days because I needed to call past associates

and ask them about our former bosses' traits and beliefs. It was not easy but it was fundamental to change my decision making and my thought processes. I needed to revisit this experiment several times to achieve the best result. An interesting habit evolved from this process, now I ask my sons or my friends, why they think what they think. I learned to eliminate stereo types from my thinking. In addition I now try think openly and avoid the pitfalls of narrow points of view. I constantly examine the origin of my thoughts and beliefs to check my decision making process. The re-creation of my decision making process was very difficult and comparable to attempting to change muscle memory.

Here I am well over five decades in age and I have decided to discover the root cause of my thoughts and actions. In this chapter I will most likely alienate the mental health industry as I did the insurance industry in chapter two. Oh well they have good coping mechanisms and they will get over it. The thought process experiment is not a game. My reminiscing about my past jobs and coworkers brought me feelings of both joy and sadness. The resulting data from my experiment cleared my decision making process which removed all

45

hesitation and doubt. Learn how to challenge your decisions. Question the status quo. Your thought and decision making processes affect every aspect of life. I compare my present way of thinking to my former way of thinking to going through life with sun glasses and then one day removing the glasses. The clarity and brightness are staggering. A change in the decision making process will result in new and maybe unfamiliar outcomes. Have you ever asked the question why do these things keep happening to me? Most likely the answer is because you consistently applied the same repetitive mental approach. Let's face it we get set in our ways yet we expect different outcomes. Predetermined mind sets will continue to cause repetitive results. Now here comes a trite term. Take yourself out of your decision making process "comfort zone."

If any of you have attended a graduate school of business in the last twenty years you have heard the term "group think." Basically it means when a group works together long enough they buy into each other's beliefs and opinions. As a group they believe they are always right. This can be a dangerous phenomenon and it can ultimately lead to failure. As was outlined in that cheerful opening

paragraph of this book, as a displaced manager or self-employed consultant you spend an inordinate amount of time alone. This can be a tricky and dangerous situation. You start to believe you know the anchor talent on CNBC personally. *Oh shucks Maria must have been on vacation this week.* One of the real dangers of the isolated environment is developing into a solo version of "group think" to "I think." There are no board meetings, no conference calls, no employee reviews or no incidental discussions at the elevator. You are alone with your thoughts and your inner voice plays like a constant Muzak loop. This is why consistent review and analysis of the origin of the thought and decision making processes is essential. At this point you are saying, *hey guy you have me playing mental games with myself and digging up the past what's the point?* The point is that we only need to look at our penal systems worst form of incarceration. Solitary confinement! The other ancillary problem with the solitary existence is that when you do get out with other live humans in a business setting you might be prone to talk too much. Be aware of this potential problem. We are social beings and the lack of interaction and intellectual stimulation has to be countered by a conscious effort on our part not to let the Jell-O settle in the mold.

Create your own inner police. What I mean by inner police is the development of a mechanism to diffuse negative processes. By freeing your mind of negative thoughts you have a better ability to move forward with your necessary tasks. Old habits die hard. Flipping your mental process may be one of the hardest things you ever do. As we discussed in chapter one it is easy to surrender to all the internal and external pressures that bombard us daily. Since we never stop thinking the mind never stops working. The voice in your head never shuts up so we need to learn to counter that voice when it is negative. It is a constant push-pull dynamic. Select a phrase that works for you to block negative thinking. A few that come to my mind are: God help me; stop; puff; not now sucker or any other phrase that draws a mental defining line the sand for you. During those times when an overdue bill or upcoming job interview causes negative thoughts depend on your phrase. Hopefully you will start to experience your self-doubt, and fears of the unknown disappear. This is not to say we should ignore our bills or minimize the importance of a job interview. What

I am saying is don't let fear or anxiety over-whelm you to a point where your mind does not function. In this way you have control over your mind rather than your mind having control over you.

We are talking about focus which is really discipline. Next we are going to talk about desire and will. The will is part of the brain. In the eighties there was a gentleman who was a genius on Wall Street. Along with his firm and his partners he was responsible for incredibly large acquisitions using the leverage buy out strategy. They enhanced the strategy by using high yield debt more commonly known as "junk bonds." These people where financial geniuses. The two principals were using privileged information to trade for personal gain. This practice is commonly known as "insider trading." Both men were prosecuted and sent to jail for few years. They both paid their debt to society but they were not welcomed back to the investment industry. After they were released from prison one of the gentlemen was diagnosed with cancer. He put his will, his talent and focuses into discovering alternative healing methods for his type of cancer. He produced great results using a common dietary product from the Far East. He was cured and he wrote a cook book designed to help people with this type of cancer. He made himself a millionaire again. This time he used his own serious illness to drive his will. The will is critical to success. I sincerely believe that this gentleman refused to be a failure even in the aftermath of a criminal conviction and while fighting a serious illness. He willed himself back to success.

During better times I was generous with my time and expertise. If a friend needed business advice or help with a business plan, I didn't hesitate to give my time to assist him/her. Now I find another uncomfortable by-product of my displaced predicament. People realize that I have time. I learned a bitter lesson. Unlike me most people won't extend an offer to help if there is nothing in it for them. I know this sounds jaded. But it angers me to think that I received no reciprocity for my kindnesses. But following my own advice I had to let go of that thought. Prior to going back to graduate school I spent seventeen years in the investment banking industry and I learned how to prepare an offering memorandum or "book" as it is known in the industry. I can also help with the preparation of debt financing and assist in raising equity want to use my education, my experience and my past reputation. I totaled the number of hours spent over the past several years on this nonsense and multiplied those hours by one hundred and fifty dollars an hour. The staggering total was one million two hundred thousand dollars. My mind is my product and they were stealing my product and I allowed it to happen. If you have a special discipline like accounting or marketing do not give it away with the hope that an opportunity can result. If a friend has a moving company and you need a sofa moved they may discount the rate but they are going to bill you. Do not give your product away. If you think a discount may get you more business than that's your business decision to make. What if you have the same precedent I did of always doing things for free when cash-flow was no object? When you are approached to do something on a success fee basis, kindly say" thanks for the opportunity but I now have a strict re-tainer requirement." Be prepared to watch your longtime friends disappear. If that's the case it's no great loss because you have pro-tected your product. In addition you will not have the regret that you have worked hard for nothing. Remember your priorities come first. When you give your time to others for no compensation your priorities slip into second place.

Our minds can be clouded. As human beings we often see what we want to see and often don't see what we don't want to see. We are living in a hyper stressful environment causing our minds to sometimes be overloaded missing what may be right in front of us. So when opportunities come about because of that they may be wolves in sheep's clothing. Sometime these wolves seek us out because we are marked as desperate and we don't realize it. We are good prey because we are hungry to get back in the game. In the next paragraph I am going to share my story.

For twenty or thirty years I functioned within the guide lines of proper business conduct. At one time I was sighted for impeccable business ethics. Unfortunately I assumed everyone else functioned in the same way. During my tenure as a member of the unemployed/underemployed/employment threatened, I spent my days talking to people, networking and trying to reignite my career. Potential business associates perceived my desire and noticed my credentials. I am a valuable person but those who might seek me out do not necessarily share my value system. I was approached by a British concern. They wanted me to manage their operation in my area. I vetted the principals as thoroughly as I possibly could on the internet. The CEO claimed to be a graduate of an Ivy League university and it checked out. Even though they are now British they are emigrants from another part of the world. At the time of my negotiations with them I had little or no exposure to their culture and therefore the business ethics of that culture. I did not want to appear to be a bigot or racist so I convinced myself to accept their offer. I was seduced by the prospect of making money. I had an uneasy feeling about the situation as well as the principals. I went against my instincts that served me well for thirty years. Believing my foreboding instincts were rooted in my ignorance I accepted the assignment. I was working sixty hours a week managing their local concern and it seemed to do extremely well. They included me in on discussions of their future acquisitions. I was thinking that my career had totally rebounded and I was collecting a paycheck every two weeks. All seemed good. A few months went by and rumors started to circulate. According to the rumor mill potential clients were upset. I asked my new employers about the rumors. They told me that the rumors were untrue. A few more weeks passed and the entity I was running was stripped of cash and thrown into involuntary bankruptcy. I don't know what happened but the company I was working for now had no money. Serious legal issues ensued for the following nine months. My involvement in the resolution of these issues depleted my mind, my body and my soul. I was thoroughly disgusted with myself for ignoring my instincts. In the end there was no rebound at all. *What does this story have to with the mind, Pat?* Everything. It demonstrates our vulnerability and craving to be a part of something. The net effect of the situation was a negative. Lawyers had to be hired, the bankruptcy had to be completed and most of all was my shame of not seeing it coming. This experience could have thrown me into a tail spin that might not have been reversible. The embarrassment of seeing my name as a witness in all the litigation procedures was sobering. Fortunately I didn't do anything wrong. But the ancillary effects of this episode took a toll on me mentally, physically and emotionally. This series of events caused me to doubt my decision making process and pushed me further into a reclusive state. The situation drained my finances, my time and my reputation. Protect your mind which houses your product. Be aggressive in your endeavors but be protective of yourself at the same time.

The state of our environment can either help or hinder our progress. The eyes see thousands of images a second and these images are registered by the mind. Keep the work area clean and neat. Two months accumulation of dust on the desk is not a pleasant picture to look at for ten hours a day. As managers we like to cultivate and grow things. But the number of coffee rings on a desk does not qualify as a quantifiable achievement. Keep your desk as pristine as you kept your desk in your office at XYZ corp. Most likely you tend to the household mail while at your desk. Set up a chronological system of what bill is due when and file it. Staring at a pile of bills all day is not healthy. After you file your bills according to due date calculate the resources available for payments. Put it out of sight and move on. Your environment, even though it may be a home office, is your corporate headquarters. It should reflect the same atmosphere of the corporate office at XYZ Corporation. Tell the family that from nine to five are your working hours. They should only interrupt you in a case of extreme emergency. You may or may not be billing during this time but the people you need to communicate with are available during these hours. They work business hours and we must work business hours as well. When on the phone with business contacts household noise should not filter through. The party on the other end of the line should not hear the television blaring, kids fighting or the dog barking. These ideas are simple but necessary to keep pressure off your mind while working.

We have a great deal of time on our hands and what we do with it is critical. Life is filled with distractions even in our solitary situations. Playing solitaire and reading the splash page of your browser that reports the goings on in Hollywood are a waste of time. These activities rob your time and drain your brain. The mind needs exercise every day. Find reading material on subjects that are new for you and that will force you to think. Challenge yourself to explore new topics and to find new solutions to complex problems. We should never stop learning. Use some of your spare time to learn something new that may help your career and enhance your life. I only had a rudimentary knowledge of Microsoft Excel. I never needed to learn it in depth because I had staff that created my Excel documents. Now as part of expanding my mind I make it a point to go over an Excel tutorial weekly. Learning Excel not only has exercised my brain but it has increased my skill level so I can now create my own spreadsheets as needed. My new practice of learning new things releases a positive energy.

Plant a rose bush. I can hear you say *damn did I waste good money or what? This guy is a whack job who wants me to plant a rose bush.* As managers we are like farmers. We plant "seeds" with our vendors, our clients and our employees. We nurture and cultivate our plantings until our efforts produce results. Every year we try to recreate our product and produce a higher yield with more efficiency. I must admit I have always dreamed of cultivating an English garden with trimmed hedges, crushed red stone paths and rose bushes everywhere. So I am starting with one rose bush at a time. I can watch the results of my efforts in the growth of my rose bush. During the course of a fiscal year companies need to hit certain bench marks. A farmer uses "knee high by the fourth of July" as the benchmark for his corn crop. The growth of the rose bush under our care represents our ability to plant, to nurture and to produce results. Growing the rose bush can give us a mental boost. It helps

Brace yourself for more support for the mind. Wake up every day at the same time. Maintain a pre-work routine. I start my day with a self-imposed sense of urgency. I am showered and shaved by eight am. I read my paper and drink coffee from eight a.m. until eight thirty a.m. I set aside some time for meditation or prayer. I find this last practice vital to the success of my entire day. At nine a.m. my work day begins. I start with my outlined agenda from the previous evening. I need regimentation. My morning routine helps me to perform calmly with sense of direction. Waking in the morning at different times and procrastinating for an hour before I shower dooms my mental outlook and will result in a lack luster day. If I sleep in until nine a. m. and do not get to work at my desk until eleven a.m. I am already defeated. For those I need to contact the morning is nearly over and lunchtime is an hour away. I realize I have wasted valuable hours and I feel guilty because my partner in the family corporation has been working for three hours. This situation produces negative energy. Set a routine and stick to it. Do not doom your chances for a successful day which only creates more stress for an overworked mind. A daily routine is nothing new for any of us we did it for thirty years.

We just spent some time looking at the decision making process and how a daily schedule and uncluttered environment help to keep us mentally focused. Now we visit another critical issue. We all have some people in our lives that have negative outlooks on life. When I discussed the depressing period before my Four Amp revelation, I mentioned my two consulting brothers and our phantom consulting firm. I said I felt like we were three trapped coal miners gasping for air. Our frequent conversations were not healthy. It didn't take studying Freud for me to come to this conclusion. It is not mentally productive to consistently participate in negative conversations. In contrast talking to positive and up lifting people improves my state of mind.

Your family shares this dilemma with you. They are adjusting to the household changes and the uncertainty is most likely scary for them. As leader of the household I need to be the pillar of positive thinking. I need to appear energetic even when I am at my lowest point. Keeping my eye on the ball I never loose site of the fact that my family is my highest priority. If my mental state appears low it can affect the mental state of the whole household. Just as it is difficult for us to find ourselves unemployed/underemployed/employment threatened it is also difficult for our partners. While we can understand and commiserate with their frustration it is not healthy for us to endure a daily brow beating sessions. This is yet another negative byproduct of this situation we find ourselves in. We need our communication to be non-combative. Sadly there will be some marital casualties. If there were relationship problems prior to the change in employment status these problems have become compounded. It is a good idea to set time aside for discussions with your significant other. It is important to be attentive and engaging in these conversations. It might be a good idea to have these discussions away from the rest of the family. Nightly negative attacks are counterproductive to a positive mental state.

It is beneficial for everybody working or not to take time for private contemplation. What I do is visualize where I want to be. *Oh geez here he goes with visualization and you thought the rose bush was bad.* For some people it works by taking twenty minutes a night and focusing on the situation that might make this period in your life worth the strife. This is a healthy mental exercise. Remember your mind is dealing with new events. You might not have had this kind of financial stress in your life before. This could be virgin territory for the CPU that is also known as your mind.

We have been discussing negative influences in regards to possible business associates and spouses. There is one more area to consider which is the extended family. Moms, dads, sisters and brothers all have their own opinions. It is human nature for them to want to share those opinions. I have learned to make it a habit to steer away from discussions about my personal business. I come from a loving family who also experienced prolonged periods of fiscal hardship. My mother worked like a dog to support the family and tried to maintain a sense of normalcy. She set the example of an uncompromising work ethic that manifested itself in all four of her children. My family's collective thought process is generally negative. Unfortunately they seem most comfortable when things do not go well. Their conversations continually center on communicating their problems and the problems of others. Sadly this has been their pattern of communication for many years. Unfortunately it probably won't change. Having been raised in this negative environment has set me up to think negatively. So I need to work extremely hard to counter my own negative thoughts. They do not realize the effects of their negativity and they do not understand the effect of their words on those around them. Since I try to make it a habit not to discuss my challenges with them, they have no idea of their destructive impact on me. For the sake of my mental health I have had to make some difficult changes. I have requested that some family members refrain from calling me during business hours. This change was necessitated because I need to focus on the wellbeing of myself and my immediate family. Sometimes it is necessary to set parameters to maintain health. If the family dog is making you crazy suggest to your family sending the dog to a nice old couple with a farm. Just kidding I love dogs. This is a serious time and creating an optimal environment to support a positive mental state is fundamental.

I am fascinated by hyper successful people who perform with seemingly effortless consistency. I am not talking about the sports stars we watch like Mariano Rivera of the New York Yankees or the splendid sounds Yo Yo Ma consistently produces from his cello. The people I am talking about are the successful when we are under extreme stress. None of these people are pretentious or braggadocios. As a matter of fact they all possess the quality of humility. You may ask me how do you think they would respond if their apple carts were turned over? They would simply set new goals and ride on their disciplined lifestyle to meet them. Where some of us might view losing a job as a near fatal career disaster people with the qualities mentioned above would see it as only a setback. On a personal note, To Tom, Jay, Tom, Ricky, Arnie, Carolyn, Jim and Marty thank you for giving me the insights I need at this difficult time in my career. Now you are ready to throw the book because for twenty years you were in the office at seven a.m. and never left before six p. m. You were the most disciplined manager at the company. Relax; I am not talking about physical discipline, which comes later in the book. I am talking about mental discipline. This can only come from continuous internal focus on your end goal and finding the best path to achieve that goal. The goal does not change from eleven a.m. and two p.m. and then revert back to the original plan. Consistency of positive thinking coupled with tight mental discipline is the secret of achieving one's goals. Allow no outer interference to break that code. External forces including a slow economy held hostage by gridlock in Washington need not be deterrents. A highly trained mental approach will always achieve the desired results. Yes we need to retrain our thought processes. This process begins with looking at how we are wired. For example, do you read something once and have it committed to memory or do you need to write information several times before it is committed to memory? Figure out your learning process. Create your individual exercise to use to assimilate new information. In the beginning this new process may take practice. This develops your form of consistent thought process. In time your new way of learning will become second nature.

We are surrounded by all types of people. Many of them are not hyper successful. We have friends and associates who are normal hard working survivors like us. I try to surround myself with good people who all have a positive outlook on life. Earlier I mentioned my friend Jim. He is a good person, almost too good. If he promises to lend somebody some money, even though he knows they are conning him, he keeps his word. His word is his bond almost to a fault. Even individuals in fiduciary positions or people in positions of trust have betrayed Jim's trust. Those individuals who cut corners are inherently negative and impede our progress. I try to seek out people in my life who are honest and positive. When it comes to friends and associates my philosophy is I prefer quality to quantity.

Now you might be a little confused, because I wrote about developing an individual process. Yep this is not a one size fits all deal. Find the medium that works best for you. For some it could be dialing the phone for others electronic social networking and even others traditional networking are the tools they use. My goal here is to model a methodology observed from great people and adapt it to the individual. So far we have talked about modifying the decision making process, creating an organized work environment, developing a disciplined thought process and formulating a solid plan. The tools are in place to work successfully towards the goal. This chapter is not meant to be a guide to self-disciplined. It is a call to self-reliance. You had the self-discipline before your psyche absorbed the negative events that led to the downturn in the economy causing so many to populate the unemployed/underemployed/employment threatened world. This is a call to your individual action. Only you can propel yourself into a new state of confidence. By reawakening and strengthening what already exists in your mind, your body and your soul you will produce quantifiable results. Reawaken and strengthen your mind so it is a valuable tool and not your path to a mental wasteland.

Alright, I have revised the origins of my decision making process: cleaned my desk, planted a rose bush, shot the dog, alienated my family, showered at seven every day, walked around the house with the iPod on and developed a consistency of thought process as well as established a goal. After about ninety minutes into my day I begin to feel like a loser because nothing has changed and I am depressed. So I take a deep breath because I know I have a few more clubs in the bag. When I experience these lows I reach back to my methodology I learned from an individual from my "quality group." This man is one of the best business behavioral consultants on the planet. He is located in Los Angeles and for the purposes of this book his name is Marty. He taught me back in 1982 when I was a young stock broker. The methodology has three components: Day One; Time Lock and Given Reality. Day

One: The meaning of the concept day one is that everything to this point is behind you and this is day one going forward. Time Lock: Time lock pertains to your work day. Block out your day and commit to every task for a defined period of time. Stay committed to the time allotted for each task even if it seems a useless exercise. Given reality: The understanding that is your situation and the only way to change it is through hard work. By the way Marty is one of those people who impart a contact high of positive vibrations every time we speak. The Wall Street firm I worked for at that time knew that if I attended one of Marty's sessions my production would increase thirty percent. They put me in Marty's presence as often as possible. What I learned from Marty helped me to develop discipline in my work day.

Ok you feel like I sometimes feel, a little bummed out. You are in the middle of everything using your new approaches and you still feel stagnate. It's ok. I can show an accidental trick I discovered one day as I prepared for an IRS audit. I was going through old files and ran across a file that I had not seen in years. As I read the contents I realized the file was filled with old reviews, press releases and awards I had received throughout my career. I am not exaggerating when I tell you that half way through the file I started to cry. Yes I realized that is the second time I talked about crying. Crying does not come easily to me (That is why I will never be Speaker of The House.) I asked myself where did that guy go? The answer is nowhere. He is still here in possession of the same talents and skill sets lauded in the contents of that file. I hope over the course of your career you have won awards or had great reviews. Hopefully you saved them. Try to find one positive review or an accolade you received in the past. Read it. Recall the source and bask in the glory of your past accomplishment. Believe me this will release positive chemicals to your brain. Be reminded of the talents and skill sets that are parts of you. Possibly since receiving those accolades your skill sets are even more developed. Here is the reality, the job left you but the talents and experiences are still there. Now how do you feel?

Now comes the true self-reliance test. Over the years we became associated with many people. Some are incredibly powerful and possibly intimidating. In some cases maybe we did not achieve mutual understanding at the time of separation. Set aside your possible negative recollections of your experiences with any of those individuals. Now make a list of the ten most powerful and influential people you ever worked with but heretofore you have been hesitant to contact. Find a reason to call them to reopen the lines of communication. Understand that at some point in your career these people saw qualities in you that prompted them to hire or to promote you. Even if you have had no contact with an individual for ten or even twenty years call him/her. I did this exercise at the beginning of my Four Amp journey. This "test" propelled me into several potentially life changing work opportunities. Now you are hot, the dog is dead, you can't go to moms for Sunday dinner and your fingers are bleeding from rose thorns and you are wondering why I just didn't say this two pages ago. Simple. The better your preparation and the less distracted you are the better your chances of a positive outcome when you make those calls. If your voice is timid and your confidence is in the garage while you are making calls from the bedroom it won't work. You have only one shot at getting the attention of these people and cannot afford to come up empty handed. That's why I didn't mention this earlier. You have a significant history with these people and it would be foolish to discard these opportunities. Even worse would be to contact them in a condition similar to my condition in chapter one. Remember they see you as you were. You need for them to retain that perception. If you are in your pajamas thumbing through the bills with the kids fighting in your office the probability of a successful call is slim. Your mind has to be in the right place to make the call and to achieve your goal. Hopefully the call produces a positive action requiring a follow up call.

Now you are proactive and it is time to put your network to work for your benefit. This may be challenging and uncomfortable at first. Networking is not a new concept to you. Only now you are networking on behalf of yourself instead on the behalf of a company. It has always been your practice to keep business out of personal social events because your friends are just that, friends. You never asked about their professional lives. The purpose here is not to use our friendships. But it doesn't hurt to tactfully inquire. The information you receive might surprise you. One day as I was networking and an acquaintance shared with me that he knew of a couple of logistic companies that were seeking an equity investor. The next day I was on the phone with the large LBO/Private Equity firm I used to work for. (The founder of this firm was one of the individuals on my ten most powerful list.) I learned that they had just closed on a large equity fund to acquire transportation and logistics companies. Wow! My planets aligned in a hurry. Do not be hesitant to ask for a fee and/or a written commitment for your services. Members of your network have needs and you have the contacts to help them support those needs. This is a good example of your mind being your product. Remember, acting on an idea may not lead to an immediate quantitative result. But it will result in an immediate positive accomplishment. Be the person in the know and a strong resource.

CHAPTER 4

The Body

"Once it gets past the lips it lands on the hips"

Some Fat Person

It is Saturday morning and I proceed to the kitchen to get my coffee. As I look around the room I see that my sons had friends over last night. And much to my delight they made frozen pizza rolls, rather than ordering expensive home delivery. I smile because they had fun and it didn't cost a great deal of money. As I sit drinking my coffee I am staring at the twelve hour old greasy pastry puffs. I reach in and eat one. I am chewing but not tasting and I am eating them as if they were a fresh order of Beignets from The French Quarter in New Orleans. I go up to shower with no true recollection of what I just ate and how it may affect my body. I have become a compulsive "picker" not even aware of what I consumed. The need to fill a void is dictating my behavior. I would never have imagined this indiscriminate eating in my former mental state. I am working from home wearing sweat pants and every trip to the kitchen results in a nervous chew. I am unaware of what it is doing to my waist line because my new daily uniform has an elastic waist band. It is time to visit the power plant we call the body. We need to get a grip on tuning the senior executive body back to high a performance mode.

I am not a psychologist, (you have to be sick of reading this by now) nutritionist or athletic trainer. I am a fifty six year old man with an athletic build, who in the depths of his employment crisis, has let himself balloon out to a disgusting size. This is so unhealthy and counterproductive as well as unappealing to any potential business associate/employer. I started to be disgusted with my reflection in the mirror but I kept giving in to eating and not caring. This could be a pretty serious issue seeing that I had a heart attack at age forty. My home is a town house with four flights of stairs. The office is located on the third floor. The hike from the kitchen to the office to get coffee during the day was becoming a truly laborious event. Making the situation worse is that I have twin twenty one year old sons who are NCAA hockey players. They cook and eat a great deal of food. They were home for the summer. The smells of bacon frying or cookies baking would be a signal to abandon my task at hand. With the excuse to get more coffee I went to the kitchen. I did not care about my health or appearance. It was reducing my usable wardrobe which was becoming another serious issue. When I was in management I was fastidious about my appearance and I liked nice clothes. As I worked up the size chart the quality of men's wear I was forced to buy was not up to my previous standards. I went to meetings looking sloppy and uncomfortable. My appearance made the person across the table feel uneasy. This was a visual sign that I was giving up and I did not care. My family was starting to get concerned about my health which only created more stress for everyone.

Earlier in the book I alluded to my cathartic Four Amp event. This event triggered actions across my entire human behavior spectrum. Quietly, the day after contemplating the Four Amps, I reduced my daily caloric intake to twelve hundred calories. I started eating the way a cardiac cripple should eat, a fist full of the right food four times a day. Four weeks later I had lost six inches off my waist. My family now laughs as I run up the stairs. I hit the tread mill at home and started lifting light weights. These activities coincided with many positive actions at my desk. I started to feel some of my old rhythm return. I started working my way back into my finer clothes. I started walking with more confidence. Then I said to myself something good has triggered inside me and I liked it.

Food is fuel for the body. I thought back to my eating habits when I was running the two companies. That thought triggered a memory of a conversation I had with a hyper success-ful client I worked with years ago. He once told me that Americans waste too many (bill-able) hours deciding on what they are going to eat for lunch. That statement stayed with me for thirty years. At the top of my game my lunch consisted of a tuna or turkey sandwich every day with no mayo or chips and a diet soda. My weight never fluctuated. I felt light and energetic. I ate a small breakfast and a sensible dinner usually still sitting on the stove because the family had eaten hours before I made it home. I was never concerned about what I ate and only recently did I realize how I let my eating habits get out of control. At this point my diet is very strict. I read content labels and I take a pass on things like diet soda due to the harmful chemicals. (Here I go again. Now I have added the soft drink industry to the mental health community and insurance industry to my list of offended industries. Oops.) By the time I reach the chapter at the end of the book the only industry not offended will be the sadly defunct space program. But I digress. Now find which foods keep the energy level high and will keep the pounds low. Even thin people need to consume foods that provide prolonged energy. Energy provides the stamina needed to traverse the slalom we call the unemployment/underemployment terrain.

A disturbing byproduct of my weight gain was my inability to walk. Due to a genetic arterial disease it was difficult for me to walk a distance as short as several blocks. Yet this condition can only be improved by walking. Go figure. When I reduced my caloric intake I started walking for short intervals and now my stamina has increased and my leg pain has been reduced significantly. Working from home is more sedentary than working in an office. We no longer walk from the train to our offices; we no longer walk the plant floor. When we work at home we wake up and shuffle to an office ten feet away from our bedrooms after slamming down twelve hour old pizza rolls. I am not saying become a work out fanatic because you do not have the time right now. Plus you cannot afford a gym membership. Do simple things like in the middle of the day put your head phones and walk around the block once after eating your power lunch. This practice is relaxing, healthy, energizing and you get some fresh air. After dinner when the dishes are clean take your significant other and go for a walk together. Without the use of headphones please. Use this time to see how he/she is holding up. It will give you an opportunity to discuss important matters outside of the kids' ear shot. Hell, it might even trigger a little romance. As we all know it is the greatest of all calorie burners known to man. *Hey Mildred, Pat says if we bump boots more often I might find a job.*

Let's consider the smoking habit. Not much to say about this because you only need to read the side of a package of cigarettes. Yes, I was a smoker and when a pack of cigarettes crested over twelve dollars in Chicago I knew it was time to quit. The best thing that I found as a substitute for cigarettes was the blue e cigarette. Yes, I still get nicotine but I don't get the tar which is the killer. The bottom line about smoking: it is a deadly, energy robbing habit and a luxury that we can't afford.

Alcohol. This is not one of my vices but I think it falls along the same lines as smoking. Excessive drinking is unhealthy, expensive and counterproductive especially at this time in our lives. This doesn't mean that sharing a cheap bottle of wine with the significant other to relax on the weekend is a bad thing. Maintain control of your faculties your family will appreciate it.

My eating is under control and I am maintaining my weight. I am walking twice a day and I am not smoking. These behaviors keep my engine pumping strong. This chapter is titled "Body" and it also encompasses appearance. You are on a budget but must project an image of confidence and success. Rank the suits or clothes that fit well from best to worst. Wear what is appropriate for a given event. Find a low price dry cleaner in your area. Try to maintain a professionally laundered shirt. If this was your practice when you had a managerial position it is important that you continue the same practice. From a practical point of view, with what is going on at home the extra chore of washing and ironing shirts can be a sense of Irritation. Then there is the possibility of a major screw up if someone forgets to do the laundry. Realizing you do not have an ironed shirt as you dress for an important meeting can be a upsetting. If when you were an executive you used to get manicures learn how to manicure your own nails. It is easy and makes you feel good. Keep yourself as well groomed as you did when you were employed. On Sunday afternoon instead of eating chips and watching television line up all your dress shoes and polish them. Yes I said you. These positive actions help you move closer to your goal. Now you think I am rose bush loving dapper Dan? No. I believe that I never want to apologize for my appearance or my punctuality. These are easy elements to control. A great manager is aware of every detail. Manage yourself to greatness. In the nineties "casual Friday" became the rage. I did not participate in this practice. I was asked by a fashion editor from a Chicago paper why I did not participate. The essence of what I said was that Friday is twenty percent of my work week. What if I accidently ran into that prospect that I have been courting for a year and he/she had a suit on? I would need to start the conversation with an apology about my casual appearance. Hell I hate golf. So why do I want to look like I play golf one day week? I won't lose my pride because I am a casualty of a faulty economic system. So why would I allow my appearance to reflect the impact of an external situation?

I realize this could be a stress-full and embarrassing time for those who find themselves unemployed/underemployed/employment threatened. At one time we felt a great deal of pride in ourselves, our accomplishments, our positions, and our organizations. It is healthy to approach life with humor and a sense of joy. Humor and joy are uplifting elixirs for the invisible brothers and sisters who find themselves unemployed/underemployed/employment threatened. There is no international brotherhood of the unemployed. There is the occasional support group for the unemployed. If they work for you that is great. This is serious. I learned a long time ago that people remember more through humor than through lecture. We need to laugh. It is free and it brings the blood pressure down. Take care of your health for the benefit of you and all those who care about and count on you.

CHAPTER 5

The Soul

"Our Lady of Victory Pray For Us"
A traditional prayer closing of
The University of Notre Dame community

I am not a psychologist, self-help guru, nutritionist, member of the clergy or a saint. I am glad I got that off my wings again. Discussions of the soul are an incredibly personal and sensitive area. For those who believe in God it is a receptacle for sin and the forgiveness of sin. Not all of us believe in God or we worship different gods in different ways. To others the soul is a recipient of rewards for the good we do in the universe. Soul for the context of this book is inner self. The reflection of how we treat our fellow man and our reactions to the successes and adversities of life. When dealt a curve ball in our otherwise blessed existences, do we let the curve ball consume us? Or do we perceive the curve ball as a minor setback in our overall life journey? We mourn the losses of salaries, perks and bonuses so we feel sorry for ourselves. Considering the big picture, do we have it so bad? Or are we reluctant to look at all the opportunities that are all around us and know we can take advantage of them? Do we ever consider the possibly that we can prosper to a greater level than in the past? We are our own best resource.

We are all emotional beings and we respond to stimuli differently. Just as we must know how we are wired to produce positive energy we must also understand our responses to anger to fear and to frustration. Our chosen responses may produce negative energy which ultimately can be extremely damaging to us, our families and our souls. Ask yourself this. What is your initial gut response to a bad situation? I know mine. And I will tell you how I know. In the early eighties I was a young stockbroker at a major investment firm. After we passed a certain threshold of assets under management, the company would put us through a series of psychological tests. There was a good reason for this practice. Management did not want brokers going crazy with other people's money. (And you thought they didn't care). One day my phone rang it was the Human Resources department located out east. They had to call me to tell me that out of approximately ten thousand brokers they tested, I tested as the most passively aggressive ruthless individual ever to take the exam. I did not know at that point if I was going to be fired or be promoted. My responses are strongly passive aggressive which can be extremely hurtful to me and those around me and especially to my soul. I know this about myself and try to avoid passive aggressive behavior. If one is prone to physically aggressive behavior that person needs to be aware of it and know how to defuse it. Learning to control your physical aggressive responses improves the soul. If alcohol and anger are causes of physical aggression professional help is needed. Without professional help a person could find himself/herself under a viaduct holding a cardboard sign. These are serious issues and the addition of stress can only exacerbate the issues. Please get professional help.

Forgiveness is an interesting concept when looking at the complexities of one's soul. On my team we need to go into the confessional to get forgiveness. That happens to be our gig. I am not necessarily talking about an overt sin or an extremely vial deed. We are living in a global economy with millions of interacting parts. The best example of that was when bad mortgages from Arizona emptied the coughers of some small remote Scandinavian farm town. We were business people and we were important, but not that important. Knowing that we did not embezzle all the corporate cash or file false documents with SEC there are a few other things we that we know: 1) We did not create the banking crises of 2008; 2) And we did not create the last recession; 3) And we were not the leading employer leaving our town for China to capture lower labor rates therefore destroying the local economies. I think you see my point. We did not cause the economic downturn and we did enact the faulty legislation. So we cannot view ourselves as the villains. Our significant other understands this, and in time our children will as well. Our souls should be light because we had no control of the external events. No need for guilt, it is too expensive of a luxury. Fault and the need to assume it or assign it is a dangerous phenomenon common in today's society. My family had a devastating business collapse when I was three years old. The loss of that business was the nightly topic of conversation for my parents. It became the family obsession and continued to be discussed until I left home at eighteen. Hearing the words loose or lost every night throughout my childhood conditioned my mind to expect failure. It wasn't until my senior year of prep school did I learn that Pearl Harbor was not my fault. Get it?

Honesty is the foundation of the soul. Often we carry feelings and emotions that are either not genuine or that are conflicted. This is a very important aspect of the soul and achieving the Four Amps. Honesty with all those you come in contact with is essential for achieving success. What is even more critical is that you be brutally honest with yourself and those you love. What is it **Bucky, you can't tell Mildred that you kissed Mary Allison Kuthacowsky at the office holiday party in nineteen ninety two? Buck did it stop at a drunken kiss?** *Yeah Pat honestly it did.* **Then I might leave that one buried Buck.** What I am talking about is the total reconciliation of your emotions with reality. This can be a difficult to achieve. However we do harbor feelings of resentment, emptiness, inequality and/or loneliness in our relationships. Fear often holds us back from reconciling these feelings with reality. To free the soul we need to rid ourselves of negative feelings. I am sure this may not be the ideal time to address critical emotional issues with career strife and financial uncertainty already increasing stress levels. You have flushed your body of fat and toxins so don't you think your spiritual/emotional health deserves the same respect? Don't your loved ones deserve the gift of honesty? Not only spouses or partners but also this is meant for our parents, children, best friends and/or all other extremely close relationships. Hopefully past dishonesty can be resolved and you can continue to grow together. Assuming they are beyond repair at least coming clean will lift that weight off you. Many of you may say hold on, I am a "not counted" unemployed person and now you want me to stir my emotional pot? No. I want you to be totally honest with those closest to you. Remember you are supposed to love each other. That brick of dishonesty on your soul, if it exists for you, needs to be lifted. Total peace is required for you to achieve your goal. Hopefully you are in a loving and honest relationship. But if you don't reconcile the negative issues in any close relationship it will prevent you from achieving the Four Amps.

Once the honesty issue is genuinely and satisfactorily dealt with, maintain open communication and respect with your partner. Recently I was talking to another "not counted" brother. He is a friend of mine who is a portfolio manager on the west coast. He is extremely successful but for one reason or another finds himself enduring his fourth year of employment exile. Richard and I are working on a project with a mutual friend who is a national expert on algorithmic stock trading. Many of you may know algorithmic trading as the "black box" or high speed trading. In the course of one of our conversations Richard asked me what's new? So I told him about writing this book and how it relates to our mutual plight. Richard and I discussed various the themes in the book. Amazingly or maybe not so amazingly, Richard was surprised to realize how themes in the book were parallel to some of his experiences. Then we then talked about the "trade" which is our mutual focus and how Richard checks his trading results daily. Richard is married to a wonderful woman who is an extremely successful engineer in the Silicon Valley. She does quite well so they are comfortable. Every day when Richard's wife comes home from work she is excited to double check Richard's trading results. So pleased is she with the trading results that she looks at him and says "I look forward to the day when I am at home with you and won't need to work anymore." What a great statement of belief and confidence in Richard's efforts. Richard's wife substantiates him every day, not just his trading results. She has input and partners in Richard's efforts. With this dynamic in place, Richard knows he is a contributor and mutual builder of their future. Stay honest and communicate with your partner and good things can happen. That is a great example of spousal validation, love, honesty and respect.

Hopefully for the past twenty five or thirty years, you have been a kind, fair and giving person to those with whom you have interacted. Now you feel that the kindnesses you afforded others are not always reciprocal. Come on you now you know I hit a nerve with that one. Guess what? It's cliché time, life isn't fair. Regardless of what your position is in life or what it may have been, act from what you know is right and never waver from your principles. Earlier I told you the story of my British acquaintances that put me in a front row seat for many legal proceedings. Before I entered into this particular business association, I wrestled with an internal conflict of whether or not to enter into a business relationship with them. They are British but they are emigrants from a region of the world where I have had little experience. As I learned from this encounter their values, mores and principles were not akin to my experiences up and to that point. Thinking that prejudice was the origin of my uneasiness I overruled my gut feeling and proceeded into a business relationship. I told myself they were well vetted and educated in some of the best institutions in the world. In the end, my sense of uneasiness about them regarding their business acumen proved to be true and it had nothing to do with where they were educated. There are good and bad people in the world, it is as simple as that. Sometimes we cannot differentiate the good from the bad because it takes time for their true colors to surface. I have to admit I was smitten with the possibilities of their offer. I hoped this association would blossom into a long term career opportunity. It did not. In the end my initial concerns were justified. What I learned from the British connection is to trust my moral compass. With that understanding under my belt I can relax and be confident in my decision making process. Never in any situation will I compromise my beliefs or values for compensation or advancement. I succeeded for many years in the cut throat business world without selling out. If I start now I will be out of the game for good. Better to be able to comfortably look into a small mirror than be ashamed in front of a large ornate mirror. Thus my soul is at peace.

In the beginning of this book I described many of my emotional responses. These responses can be separated over three emotions: anger; jealousy and fear. You remember I mentioned driving to a lunch that I had scheduled with a self-centered blowhard associate. As I drove through the business district I recalled how I felt when I was a vital part of this community. Initially my response was to get upset as I recalled the time that had past and I started to regret every subsequent decision I made. I felt angry, sad and betrayed. I learned that the need to control those responses is vital to my survival. Functioning in a constant state of resentment and anger is not productive. Instead of remembering the people I hired and trained for their betterment I chose feelings of anger and resentment. I forgot all those successes only to fall into a deep feeling of inadequacy. I do not have the resources or the luxury of time to allow myself to participate in negative emotions. I told myself to snap out of it and to remember when that branch set a district record for production or of fear resulted in the conditioned response to flee. I allowed an imagined perception to create a mental situation that may or may not have been accurate and then I negatively reacted to it. I needed to ask myself this question. Why did the presence of this unsuspecting person create any kind of response from me? It goes to my negative emotional state which depletes the energy of my soul. It comes down to my choices. I can choose to see a well-dressed professional looking person and go with negative feelings or I can choose to focus on positive stimuli. This takes a great deal of emotional awareness and discipline. *Damn Pat this is one big convoluted mess of wires like the wires behind the home entertainment system hiding in the dust.* **Good analogy Buck.** Now you know why the origins of your emotional responses are critical. Sadly, due to the example of my father's negative emotional responses I inherited the habit of creating therefore assuming a defeatist attitude. I needed to re-learn to pattern my emotional responses from positive people. Positive responses most likely result in success. I have revised my historical pattern of emotional response processes by observing the processes of the eight calm successful people that I mentioned earlier. Our emotional responses are the starting points for most of what we proceed to do. If we begin with anger, fear or jealousy positive outcomes are nearly impossible. If the initial reaction is hopeful, confident and a willingness to seek understanding of the unknown success is likely follow. Look out. Getting out of your own way may enhance your success.

We live on a planet with millions of others and we share the air, water and land. If you live in a major metropolitan city you walk by thousands of nameless strangers every day. Each person has a story and possibly a cross to carry. When we are faced with quasi isolation the majority of our thoughts can become about ourselves. We are prone to self-absorption and the myopic view that no one else has our difficulties. I do not mean to diminish the frustration, embarrassment and angst that a person in our situation endures hourly. But let's gather some perspective. Did you wake up with a tag on your toe this morning? That is a good start. I promise not to parrot my loving family's form of solace by telling you how much worse the rest of the world is. I will tell you to take inventory of the good that surrounds you. As we have seen so far the soul is a powerful force. It can propel you or it can debilitate you in a matter of seconds. I mentioned the concept of taking inventory of the good. By that I mean the positive elements in your life. A loving partner who is willing to roll up his/her sleeves and makes sacrifices; great children; a good education; and most of all freedom to carve out your own place in this great country. Now look at ninety nine percent of the planet. How are you doing? If your situation caused the breakup of your marriage you are blessed because you are not living in a negative relationship any longer. Your soul, if you are true to it, gives your perspective and guidance. Assuming you have a strong value system and moral compass your soul will help lead the mind and body to a better place.

For years I have been supporting philanthropic causes, always giving of my time and my financial resources. Now I often feel cheated that that part of my life is on hold. However if I think about it I don't need to feel that way. Maybe my wallet is thinner but my compassion has grown. I still have some free time to participate in charitable activities. For example I still volunteer as a hockey coach and enjoy motivating young players who want to strive for a college hockey career. I use my time with them to plan their high school curriculum, talk

Another time when it was difficult for me to maintain any form of positive emotional state was when the IRS was hounding me about a three year old tax return. Even though the mortgage was paid but the property taxes were not. This was a tough period in my life. It was during this time that I needed to reach deeper into my soul for guidance, strength and direction. Here is a reality check. Unless Uncle Phil dies tomorrow and leaves me a bundle I'm doomed. Imagining the death of a beloved relative or any other farfetched solution is not a positive response nor is it an answer. It is my challenge to figure out how to manage my situation. The brain is thinking and the vital organs are still functioning but under extremely high levels of stress. Here is where I needed dig deep and really find out what I was made of. The IRS was threatening to garnish my partner's wages and put a brick on what was left in our savings account. My mind was racing, my heart was pounding I was almost at a full blown panic attack. This is where my soul kicked in and it started to relax me and bring me back to center. My mind became more coherent and I started to find solutions. One possible solution was the sale of assets. Also I remembered the favors I did for a corporate accounting firm. One favor involved the timely payment of invoices. I started to formulate a plan and therefore managed the IRS situation using my mind, body and soul. Trust me there isn't much I have not overcome in the past few years from serious legal issues to the IRS. I know how to figure it out. Believe me I was not happy to find myself in those situations but their resolutions gave me a huge sense of satisfaction. I am still a good, strong resourceful manager.

Your children need to see your internal strength that emanates from your soul. They will learn from your courage. Even in these challenging times, we are trying to educate and prepare our children for prosperous and successful lives like we have. Yes I said like we have and **I heard what you called me Bucky, and contrary to popular belief mother is not half a word, shame on you.** The lessons of internal fortitude, moral guidance and the unwillingness to surrender are qualities I learned from my mother. I am not go into detail but as you already know I grew up in an extremely financially challenged household from the age of three to the time I moved out at eighteen. I learned at a very young age from observation that you keep your word, work hard and if you truly believe in yourself you can solve any problems except health issues. Even under a cloud of negativity these qualities were passed on. I can only imagine what the results would have been if these qualities existed in a positive emotional environment. Teach your children there is no crime in sacrifice and there is no shame in the unbridled belief in oneself even in times of extreme stress and adversity. We always hope and pray that our children have better lives than we had. For that is the true measure of our success. But they must be equipped with all the tools to survive. Believing that the Good Lord will guide you is how some may interpret this and some may believe that the universe will show them the way. It really doesn't matter which you choose. What matters is a mechanism that triggers an inner sense of calm and confidence when faced with adversity so you can successfully respond. The glue that makes this happen is your soul. This is the best legacy you can give to your children.

We refuel our souls through prayer, meditation, reflection and service to others. Normally we are never at a loss for quiet time during the week because hell we are alone in a room. The need to take fifteen or thirty minutes a day for reflection or to put things in perspective is vital to maintaining balance and focus for the tasks ahead of us. Before I start my day I take ten minutes at my desk to review how I am managing my life. It is kind of a moral compass check list. If you haven't figured it out yet from the earlier University of Notre Dame quote, I am Roman Catholic as well as a University of Notre Dame graduate. You are now shouting to your wife *Hey Mildred an author from Notre Dame and he doesn't mention the place until Chapter five, when I would have expected this information in the first* sentence. Can you believe it? I do hold the institution dear to my heart and it is a very special place. Back to my morning routine. After my reflection, I say a series of prayers from a St. Jude prayer book given to me by my mother. St. Jude is the patron Saint of hopeless causes. That half hour really focuses me and truly makes me feel less alone. It does not matter to whom or what you pray or if you pray at all. Maybe to meditate on your interactions with your fellow man is sufficient. The point is to take the time to examine your driving force or your compass so to speak because that compass needs to work over time in the course of your day. This activity will assist you with your abilities to forgive, to forge ahead and to love. Those are some pretty heavy emotional responsibilities that present themselves repeatedly under the most trying circumstances. You may be an atheist and not believe in a deity but you still love, you still forgive and therefore often rely on some form of emotional driver. This is not about religion it is about the state of your soul.

Hey guess what? After all that, you are still going to get upset and gnarly during the course of the day. Yep we are not perfect and we have emotions and limits due to frustration and disappointment. Emotions are strong and you can let them expand your aorta or you can harness that energy and let it work for you. Unfortunately with my medical history I can't take what's behind door number one very often. But occasionally getting mad can be a good thing. It is better to bounce off my cell of an office because someone did not see the merit of my idea rather than staring at the computer screen playing solitaire or aimlessly surfing the internet. Anger about a positive action is great; anger about wasting another day is not great. The good anger shows me that I am back in play. Way to go! I still get frustrated. Only now, it is because I thought of a good person to call and I cannot remember the name of his/her company. It beats getting frustrated about not starting my day until eleven a.m. Now don't take it out on the family. You cannot kick the dog because you have already killed it. (Just kidding). To regain my composure I look internally for guidance which I believe leads me to more positive actions. At dinner I feel tired but for a good reason. I know I put in a full day in the office and my efforts give me a sense fulfillment. My family sees a glimmer of the old me. Operate for five consecutive days letting your soul be your compass and driver and see how good you feel by Friday. I bet you may have some quantifiable results.

Some people enjoy structured worship and others do not. There is no right or wrong here just personal preference. The need to take a prolonged period of self-reflection on the weekend is not a bad idea. Analyze what you did and did not do and how you might improve on some emotional responses or how you can channel negative energy into positive energy. Try this exercise. You are watching a mental game film of your previous week. Maybe for some Church is the place for that reflection. Or maybe for someone else the hammock in the yard next to the rose bush could be the reflection site. The important thing is to take the time to reorganize your mental files and charge your emotional driver. (Notice I did not say "take some time to smell the roses," oh I hate that saying). Reconnect with your family in a less hectic way than on a Thursday night when Suzy is running off to dance class and your oldest has a term paper due. Truly show an interest and probe them as to how their week went. Ask what is paramount in their lives at the moment. Implement these practices and you will be a recharged financial mercenary on Monday morning. Now here is a unique idea. In fact I do this myself. Shut your mind down on Sunday other than polishing your shoes. Shut it down, try and forget about the upcoming bills, calls to be made and appointments to be kept. Give it a rest it is Sunday but do the shoes. All the shoes!

I believe we all have a soul. It is difficult to define and it does not show up on an x-ray but it is an important part of our being. The soul is what drives people to accomplish great and heroic acts. Tell me that the soldier who in a split second jumps on the grenade and saves four lives while sacrificing his own life is not driven by a moral driver or internal compass? Tell me the social worker who walks into rat infested buildings to check on the wellbeing of another person does not have a moral driver or compass? We all use our internal compasses every day to care for our fellow man. Maybe our actions are not as unselfish but they are just as important. We need to recognize and respect the power of our souls. Those who ignore their souls come up empty in times of crises. What we do with our moral driver is important to our families and those close to us as well as all humanity. Use it. Let it flourish to assist mind and body.

We are on this planet for a very short time and we won't be remembered for our financial prowess unless our first name is Warren. We will be remembered for our actions. Suzy will tell her children that back in 2013 things were rough but somehow daddy kept her in Tony Country Day School. Things were tough that year but every night mom and dad held hands and went for a walk. We lost the landscape service but dad did the neatest thing – he planted a rose bush and buried the dog under it (just kidding about the dog again). My dad taught me how to respond to a difficult situation. He taught me to choose a positive response. He did not tell me how to respond but by his example I learned how to

CHAPTER 6

Coordinating mind, body and soul to function at Four Amps

"Ideas must work through the brains and the arms of good brave men, or they are no better than dreams"
Ralph Waldo Emerson

I am not a psychologist, self- help guru, nu-tritionist, personal trainer, clergy member, saint or astronaut. I think by now you have fig-ured that out but it's fun to reiterate anyway. I am a simple man who like you has been try-ing every method to change my unemployed or underemployed standing in this "great" economic recovery. I previously discussed a weekend of great despair when I listened to a small score of music on a sunny Saturday in Chicago. This music motivated me to my Four

Amp revelation. I was not concerned that my family would think that I finally lost my last marble. Also I was not ashamed to share this process I call the Four Amps with my friends. I realized that modeling great acts can only produce great results. I did not go to the National Space Museum and try to recreate a reentry strategy. What I did do was I imagined what focus and determination could accomplish. I emulated the sheer raw determination and discipline required to return three astronauts from space in a crippled space craft. The following day still listening to the musical score I began to adopt the Four Amp philosophy to my life. In a short time I had outlined my credo of how to reach my Four Amps by using my mind, my body and my soul. Soon I had a plan of action and strategies to reverse my direction. Up to this point I had been operating in a fog of insecure clutter and feelings of inadequacy. If my initial attempts failed I would not be deterred I would try others. The sleeping beast woke up. I met my new boss and it was me.

Often the problem with good ideas is that they never become positive actions. It is strange sometimes that a good push comes from an unexpected source. My oldest twin son called

me out. He reminded me of my advice to himself and his twin brother. His brother had just
completed his freshman year at a college out
east and he also had a great year as an ice
hockey goaltender. He succeeded in making
the conference all-rookie team. So his year
was successful not only academically but ath-
letically. I thought he was happy. But in truth
he really wanted to get back to the Midwest
to be closer to his family. During his freshman
year my financial situation prohibited me from
traveling to see a game. The problem with
transferring schools is that there are only one
hundred and sixty NCAA hockey programs.
Yes there are several hundred club teams but
it has always been both boys' dream to play in
the NCAA and they achieved their goals. With
one hundred and sixty programs and each
team carrying roughly three goaltenders that
means there are roughly four hundred and
eighty goaltender positions available. If you
take into consideration the four class years
maybe the total number of NCAA goaltender positions available in a given year is one
hundred and twenty. He was ready to give
up because very few schools had goaltender
openings. He was ready to walk away from
his life's passion and move on. So we went
online and researched every NCAA hockey

This book is about how a common man, struggling in our unemployed/underemployed/employment threatened environment, grabbed himself by the ankles and lifted himself out of a desperate situation to one of positive actions, results and individual achievement. Since my revelation I give my all to everything I do. Quickly this lifestyle is becoming second nature. My energy level hasn't been this high in twenty years. I feel like a super hero at a Wizard of Oz convention. I feel like a tall guy in blue tights and a cape walking among the munchkins. My entire outlook has changed. I feel in control of my destiny and I am relaxed. My day is spent planning and analyzing my approach to realize the next opportunity. For the first time in years I count the hours until Monday morning. As you already know the first step in my new approach was to make a list of the ten most influential people I have known in my career. On the Friday before my revelation if anyone had told me to call these people I would have refused. I would have had many excuses not to call my former high level business associates. As I made the list I remembered that at some point in my career I had some quality or characteristic that made me appealing to these people. Those qualities and characteristics still exist. My lunar landing module may be damaged but the rest of the craft is flying fine.

On Monday morning I was up at seven o'clock and at eight o'clock I was sitting behind my desk. The first thing on my agenda was to resurrect my habit of reading the journal. Next I did a bit of last minute preparation and then I started to contact the people on my list. The first call was to a management consulting firm on the west coast. I had a good history with this firm. Expecting to leave a message for the CEO, I was surprised when the receptionist answered and took my name. Ten seconds later I heard this incredibly receptive voice ask "where the hell have you been for the last seven years?" His voice was full of excitement and enthusiasm. The call had been patched through to his home in Malibu. We made an appointment for a more detailed call later that afternoon. At the appointed time my phone rang. This was a real shot in the arm for me and I was off to races. My second call was a bit scarier. I had been president of a company owned by a prestigious Wall Street LBO (leverage buy out) firm. The chairman was extremely upset in 2004 when I decided to resign. The relationship has been a little strained over the years. I know that the president and

CEO liked and respected me. While doing my research I noticed that the company made a certain acquisition last January. I knew of a few companies that may be for sale that would complement their acquisition very well. So I called the president and CEO. His secretary asked my name and purpose of the call. She took my detailed message. Twenty minutes later the company's CFO returned my called. I worked with this person fifteen years ago but there has been no communication between us for the last nine years. I picked up the phone and she said "Hi Pat, Tom asked me to give you a call. What do you have?" During that conversation, I was the steward of my mind, my body and my soul. At that moment it was my responsibility to maximize my internal harmony to achieve results. Positive momentum was created. The CFO and I started exchanging potential strategies and opportunities as if we had talked last week.

That day I began to create my health benchmarks. I ate tuna for lunch and I started counting calories. My demeanor went from despair to the hope for positive long term change. Each positive action reinforced the next. Soon a positive chain reaction started in my mind, in my body and in my soul. The deeper and more interesting my discussions became in regards to my career efforts, the less I ate and the more receptive I was to putting positive ideas into action. In management terms my internal changes were akin to when the shipping dock runs on time, the production through put hits quota which allows sales to be more aggressive. The physical corporation I call myself was clicking like the factory I just described. One day does not create change. It is however the first brick in the foundation of behavior modification.

Now the question was can I string together a few of these positive days and go on a winning streak? The next day was filled with a great deal of back and forth with the LBO firm. We discussed opportunities. We started talking about the possibility of a business structure between them and me. Soon it seemed that a possible business arrangement would be in the offing. They were viewing me as a contemporary with the same business acumen I demonstrated when I left the organization nine years ago. They referred to my company (me) and the use of my organization's standard legal documents. I am sure their perception was not of an unemployed guy in his bedroom office. But what they did know was that they were talking to a businessman who relies on himself to accomplish every task connected with his business concerns. I was excited. I was barely aware that I had slipped back into senior manager mode. In the ensuing weeks, the pace quickened and plans became projects. The bricks in my foundation have multiplied. My entire demeanor changed. My voice sounds confident, my thoughts are well organized and my results are positive. The total state of myself is improving. No longer do I obsess about my plight as an unemployed/underemployed/employment threatened person but rather I focus on individual positive opportunities.

Starting with the cathartic event on my balcony on a Saturday by the end of that first week my total approach did a one hundred and eighty degree turn. My lifestyle changes have restored my dormant instincts. At every meal I make the right choices leaving me physically less sluggish. I now walk for exercise. Every evening I approach my plan for the following day with research and an attention to detail. Each morning I wake up at the same time. Belted trousers have replaced the elastic waist band. The few changes I made set repairs in motion on my lunar landing module.

As this phenomenon continued my wardrobe expanded and my calendar began to fill. My focus changed from one of just survival to one of growth and success.

I took some time to reflect on what was happening to me. Again I thought of the astronaut Ken Mattingly and his approach to the most defining moment of his life. The lives of three friends were at stake. Two of those men had wives and children. The reputation of his country's space program was at risk. If his effort to save "Apollo Thirteen" failed it would have been the United States second fatal space disaster in the span of a few years. Mattingly was focused. His decision making process needed to be solid while maintaining the willingness to stay and fight to keep three other astronauts alive. What would I have done in a similar situation? Then I realized I am in similar situation. I am fighting for the lives of my family and myself. I do not wish to compare my situation to that of the averted "Apollo Thirteen" disaster. I am simply drawing parallels to two elements of that event. The first was my realization (through the "Apollo Thirteen" musical score) that I needed to find my Four Amps. Secondly, using the example of Ken Mattingly, I needed to be focused, determined and willing to fight to the finish. Ken Mattingly would not have succeeded if he was not in top physical condition, top mental condition and top emotional condition.

The few changes I have made produced quantitative results. The following experiment will prove my thesis. As I mentioned earlier I was in the investment industry for several years. My career started as a runner on the Chicago Board Options Exchange in the days of its origin. I had the opportunity to learn good trading skills and strategies from many brilliant and generous mentors. Stock options have never left my blood. I have tried always to have some type of trade working. Over the past few years, while under career siege, I would trade from time to time. The results were not as good as they should have been. Working with finite resources maybe this was not the best time to speculate. As my transformation was evolving I decided to challenge myself. I took one thousand dollars to trade. I decided to be truthful with myself. I did the complete opposite of what I usually did when I traded in the market. This is called "fading" yourself in the industry. In the following three weeks I made seven thousand dollars going against my historical belief system and using my new decision making process. Now I try to approach situations from a new and unique point of view and it is working. By tweaking my emotional health I created a form of spiritual peace and confidence allowing my decision and thought processes to flourish. Gone are the traditional guide lines and preconceived outcomes. I have the energy and confidence and spirit of a younger man. Not only do I see these changes in myself, those close to me see them as well. I approach every day, event, task, conversation, and thought as if I have to find Four Amps.

The weeks continued to produce positive progress marked by quantifiable results. I found myself over loaded with work and at times even frazzled. Being that I am a one man band and responsible for every task my days are quite full. Even in the most frenetic moments I smile rather than give into frustration. Managing the household finances including rapidly approaching college tuition, I still have some challenges which are a part of life. I still work at approaching each situation, whether positive or negative, with a spiritually uplifted attitude. I know that my new confidence will bring me to positive outcomes. Gone are the historical fear and long lasting angst. I am in control of a nimble decision making process and I feel extremely fit. I am in control of my destiny. By choosing a positive emotional state my decision making process has been modified for the better. One musical event triggered a major change in my entire approach to life. While this might sound funky or weird I think it's kind of cool.

The event that capped off my transition was driven by actions I committed to early in this process. I was negotiating a contract with the LBO firm. They asked me what business entity would be named in this contract. My response was that I would get back to them. At the same time a second long term project began to come to fruition. It also needed the creation of a separate business entity. I quickly called my attorney and he set up two separate LLC's (Limited Liability Corporations). Then I ran to the printer and had business cards made up for both entities. As soon as I returned home I called the LBO firm and gave them the name of the entity so we could move forward with the contract. After years of searching for a job comparable to my previous positions, only to endure rejection and embarrassment, I stood up at my desk and shouted "I am Patrick M. Palella and I am my new boss!" My family came running to the den because normally I am reserved when I work. That was my moment of awareness and proof. Knowing how I felt at that moment I could only imagine the feelings at mission control when "Apollo Thirteen" successfully reentered earth's atmosphere. Yes I may never again have the big corner office with all the perks. But I have something stronger and more durable. I have the gift of my Four Amps.

Since my awakening I have shared the Four Amps approach with family members and a few close friends and associates. The reaction has been mixed. My sons thought it was interesting and that it had potential. I am curious to see if they have applied this approach when I review their grades and observe their performance on the ice this fall. My new partners from Phantom Consulting are becoming strong advocates of the Four Amps. The older gentleman had an open mind. He said he would try anything to start making some money. He is receptive and very energetic to help with the project. The other member of phantom Consulting was more direct. He jumped on board and assisted me with the Four Amp website and all the links needed to create a social networking presence. Interestingly several of my successful and gainfully employed friends were fascinated by the Four Amp approach. They continue to ask me questions about how I feel and about my holistic progress. My friend Jim, who witnessed my melt down, bought into it. He understands it and uses the process daily. When he concludes a phone conversation with me, he closes by saying "Four Amps brother Four Amps." Energy is vital to action. If you are too tired to do anything because you are out of shape both physically, emotionally and mentally nothing gets done. Now try to focus on the improvement of mind, body and soul and see how you feel.

Not everyone reaches the hat-trick of desperation that I did. Some may work out daily and be very fit but still wrestle with confidence and decision making dilemmas. These are lucky folks because they are a third of the way there. If you have a good positive outlook and you are still off your game, a little fine tuning may be necessary. Here is my point. Awareness of what may be needed on an individual basis to change a desperate situation to a winning situation is the first step to achieving your Four Amps. The world as we know it may be gone forever. But the skills, traits and habits that brought us success in the past are still alive in us. Make improvements to your physical, emotional and mental self to rekindle the use of your skills, traits and habits that still exist within you. A good you today is better than waiting for a great you in a year. Celebrate the little victories in life.

Things are moving swiftly in the right direction. I am extremely visible at home. The evidence is noticeable to my family. We are a stronger and more confident family unit. Your family looked at you with confidence when you were the president of XYZ Corporation. Do they look at you in the same way now? Again I return to the movie "Apollo 13." When the imminent danger of the "Apollo Thirteen" craft became public knowledge, the media gathered at flight commander Jim Lovell's home where all the flight crew families were assembled. Adding to the already incredible pressure on these families was the presence of the media. Their task was to monitor the families. A reporter approached Lovell's elderly mother and asked her how she felt. She confidently replied something to the effect that "if they could get a wash machine to fly, her Jimmy could land it." Our families' confidence in us is rooted in their faith in our strength and abilities. From here on everyday your family will watch you effortlessly land your wash machine.

CHAPTER 7

No Excuses

*"Man must be arched and buttressed
from within; else the temple will
crumble to dust"*
Marcus Aurelius Antoninus

In the investment community they use two terms, systemic and non-systemic risk to describe different types of risk factors. Systemic risk refers to risk of a large, external and intertwined community. An example would be that the European economy is weak. So the pressure on the global economy forces stocks lower. Non-systemic risk is inherent to a certain entity. For example XYZ pharmaceutical company's patents on certain drugs expire and so the competition can manufacture generic equivalents. The generic equivalents will hurt XYZ's earnings next year. One is a large global event and the other only affects one company or one industry. We can apply this method of viewing risk to our daily experiences. We need to be able to differentiate between the two types of risks or shocks and respond accordingly. The internal or non-systemic risk could be controllable. But the systemic risk, which is aligned to the political system that affects us, is uncontrollable. Learn to recognize what you can control and what you cannot.

We live in a nation that counts everything from the number of hotdogs a man can consume in an allotted period of time on a July day in New York City to the number of times a president says the word "poor" during his state of the union address. From sports averages to the statistical percentage of a drug's side effects we count them. We are captivated with numbers and statistics. So much so that we have the Bureau of Labor Statistics, The Congressional Budget Office and the ultimate bean counters our friends at the Internal Revenue Service. We produce reports and forecasts for every possible crop, situation, disease, trend and useless item. We love our numbers so much that even with the use of the best technology in the world we still have to revise them thirty days later because we messed up the first time. *Hey Mildred sounds like Pat is going on a little anarchist rant in this chapter!* **No Buck, I love this country and I am just pointing out the facts.** The only number counters that think they get it right the first time are the IRS. If I forget to claim fifty bucks from a consulting job they find it. Yet all the other critical data points need revision. Go figure! No pun intended.

At the writing of this book there are 316,418,000 Americans. The true unemployment rate is really six percent higher than the government reported 7.4%. The Federal Reserve is going to use the 7.4% unemployment rate to calculate a major monetary policy decision. What is of even more concern is that the current Labor Force Participation Rate is at a thirty year low. Not to mention the 23.6 million underemployed Americans and the 14.4 million recent college graduates who cannot find employment in their fields of study. Let's do some math shall we? Six percent multiplied by 316 million equals roughly 20 million "not counted" unemployed Americans. In addition there are another 23.6 million underemployed Americans. The voice of my graduate school economics professor rings in my ears saying "full employment numbers reflect a five percent unemployment rate." (Generally speaking 95% employment is considered full employment in the United States.) I know Jeff but we are a long way from that data point. He will be happy I used his real first name.

How dare you not count us! We are all fighting to survive and to maintain the American dream. We are "not counted" because some arbitrary bureaucratic benefit period expired. A benefit some of us never received. We are "not counted" because we do not check into an office once a month to tell a clerk about our job searches. The invisible unemployed include veterans, teachers, health care professionals and business people. We have families, responsibilities and dreams. For decades we have been responsible contributing citizens. Some of us don't even take advantage of the benefits that the government provides. What we do want is the system fixed. If we would be counted the falsehood of the economic recovery would be uncovered. If the unemployment rate is thirteen percent, than it is thirteen percent. That is one of those funny little government statistics like when they exclude the price of food and energy from the inflation index. I might be extremely extravagant but I find it a little difficult to live without food or energy. Hey Ben before you continue to pump our kid's future into the bond market maybe you should know the true untold story. Buy a tabloid to get the real scoop on where the American labor statistics are. It is ridiculous that we celebrate the creation of minimum wage part time jobs while sixty percent of the unemployed/underemployed/employment threatened do not show up anywhere in the statistics. Which leaves us out of the decision making process. Earlier in this book we discussed individual fiscal assessment. Isn't it time for a national fiscal assessment? Economic stimuli like the quantitative easing one, two and three (Quantitative easing is a monetary policy in which the United States purchase its own debt in the market with borrowed funds) are not solutions to conducive, independent economic growth. Pumping eighty billion dollars a month in to the mortgage back securities market while hedge funds front run to buy residential homes only to pump and dump the properties at huge profits. This is another practice of artificially supporting an economy not conducive to individual economic growth. I am not a psychologist, nutritionist, personal trainer, economist, member of the clergy but I grew up on the trading floors and in the offices of Wall Street investment houses and I do know the capital markets. This is not working! We are a long way from the need for TARP (Troubled Asset Relief Program) and the banking crises of 2008. Yet five years later we continue to artificially prop up an economy with stimuli to garner a paltry two percent growth rate. Help us help ourselves. Take the shackles and training wheels off the economy so the forty million plus of the "not counted" unemployed and underemployed Americans can elevate themselves to help spur true economic growth.

Am I whistling in the grave yard? Let's examine some facts about our present environment. Time for a joke. What is the difference between senators and congressmen and the "not counted" unemployed? They don't work either but they still collect a paycheck and receive benefits. I could just imagine if the CEO and his key people approached the board of directors of a company that is in a critical situation and might be shut down. They tell the board that their holiday recess starts the next day. After the forty five day break they will deal with the problems. What do you think would happen to the CEO and his key people? I think there is a high probability they would join the ranks of the "not counted" and hopefully buy this book. Imagine a CFO telling the board of directors about the purchase of a new health care plan. When asked about the contents of the plan, he/she admits that he/she has not read it. What do you think would happen to that CFO? Sound familiar? Have we not seen two similar situations in this country in the last thirty six months? One of the most depressing things about prolonged unemployment is the need to stay current with news of the day. Many of us are in the habit of keeping the television on continually. That could be eight to twelve hours of repetitive news. On the other hand the average working American probably watches the news for maybe one to two hours a day.

We watch our troops in a foreign country with a reporter embedded in the Humvee. I started to think about the development of the news cycle over the past one hundred and fifty years in this country. At the time of the Civil War we had telegraph and newspapers. The type in newspapers at that time was manually blocked. The news would often come days after the event and be a relatively short account of the event. With the dawn of the radio, news came to us faster however it was still not visual. Newspapers were still the main source of news. There was still a time delay between the news event and the reporting of the event. Facts comprised the content of the news reports. News reels came in the early twentieth century. Since movie theaters were the venues for news reels the public viewed them infrequently. News reels were well-choreographed. With the television twenty four hour news cycle of today it would be impossible to conceal Franklin Roosevelt's wheel chair. During the sixties and seventies the television news aired several a times day. Even in that period reporters were more focused on the content of the news. Time did not allow reporters to editorialize. Now let's fast forward to our present day news schedules. News is reported as it happens from all over the globe. Political biases and opinions taint the facts of the stories. It seems now rather that reporting news, television news is in the business of selling a certain point of view depending on the political beliefs of stations and/or reporters. The news programs have reduced the political process of this country to a parlor game. It is more important to root for one side than it is to come together for the betterment of all. The contestants (political figures and network consultants) are given a ten second sound bite to chirp about their opponents. Rarely do they offer substantive information or solutions. These discourses have added to the polarization of this great country. We are so distracted by competition or the perceptions of fairness or unfairness that we have strayed far from the real issues and their real long term impact. Rather than talking about issues important to the advancement of this country, we are inundated with useless personal facts about political celebrities. In the meantime our political system is decaying, our infrastructure is rotting and our national self-esteem is low as we move farther from the self-reliant attitude that made this country great. News reporting should be used for information not indoctrination or persuasion.

The truth is that most of us know more about fixing an ailing entity than the people in office. We have built them, have maintained them and have repaired them. After educating ourselves we built careers from the ground up. We lived in an environment conducive to success. We overcame fiscal challenges, strong competition and restrictions in business. We worked through wars, recessions and the threats of terror. Through all of the challenges we added value to the nation's economy. The "nation's economy" is the business of the nation. I realize it is a little more complicated than running a company but basic business tenants apply. Our leaders have ignored the concepts of budgeting, fiscal constraint and responsibility in times of crises. This is a frustrating situation to those of us who still want to contribute. We are not utilized and most of all we are "not counted".

We have become a country of political junkies. We pull for a side or team in the same way we pull for our fantasy football league teams. We have news on demand twenty fours a day and we can even observe the legislative halls all day long. Beating the other team has become more important than solving national problems. Our national perspective is lost. Opposing agendas have eradicated the meaning of government by the people. The people no longer even understand the platforms of the parties.

This is not a partisan issue. Personally, I am getting a little fed up with entire cast of characters. Ampage knows no political affiliation. We have one leader who spends too much time in the tanning booth and needs to wash his hair with no more tears shampoo. The other leader bounces down the stairs of his plane returning from yet another golf junket

or vacation. He always struts sporting an Alfred E. Neuman grin. (A reference to the Mad
Magazine cover guy). The bottom line is nothing is getting done. Watching a few hundred
people pretend to work is very frustrating for a
person craving to work. We have an artificially
supported economy. The growth is a paltry
two percent. Our nation is polarized. And we
sit on the side lines wanting only to be a contributing citizen.

It is incredible that the political system and the
slanted news reports have separated us. This
separation has caused polarization. Americans resent their fellow Americans: The rich
versus poor; union worker versus independent
business person; young versus old; north versus south; east versus west and urban versus
rural. Not a pretty picture. The talking heads
in Washington manipulate demographics
so well that they put the advertising firms on
Madison Avenue to shame. One of the United
States' most powerful weapons in World War
II was the unity of this country on and off the
battle field. We will use paratroopers as examples. It didn't matter to trooper one who
was a union worker from Ohio that trooper
number two was an independent businessman from New York. What mattered was that

they were Americans with a common goal. It made no difference what their occupation was, what part of the country they called home or their political affiliation. They were Americans united to defeat the Axis powers. These brave people were strangers but were willing to die for one another. Contrast the World War II scenario to the present. We have become a country of rigid classifications each with its own agenda. Each group is so myopically focused on its own agenda that compromise for the common goal is out of sight. We don't notice the shell game in Washington because each faction is too busy condemning the other. We need to be Americans first before union workers, before independent business people before being a northerner, before being a southerner, before being a democrat and before being a republican.

So here we sit "not counted" a rotten term to describe a terrible and frightening position. We were counted when we waited their tables while putting ourselves through school. We were counted when we worked as domestic help as we cleaned their homes to pay for learning a trade. We were counted when we paid our student loans. We were counted when we had six digit incomes and they wanted our tax payments and political donations. I will not swear in this book but, #@%^&* off and count yourselves as inept parasitical elected government employees. I have an idea. A year before the next national election the "not counted" should identify the most crucial battle ground state. Contact a friend and/or relatives and establish residency in that state. What would twenty million additional voters in Ohio do to the voter turnout in that state? Truly that scenario would baffle the pollsters. How could anyone predict the "not counted" vote? The aid would say what's "not counted." The pollster says the "not counted" voter. This could be better that Abbott and Costello's, "Who's on First". We could make the "not counted" matter!

By now you might be totally confused and totally angry. You are yelling at *Mildred saying this son of a gun. I bought into this positive crap for five chapters, planted a rose bush, organized my thoughts, called former clients, killed the dog, went on a diet, enrolled in yoga and now in this chapter he dumps this bucket of garbage on my head.* **Relax Bucky. I have some bad news and some good news for you. Seeing that you are incredibly hacked off anyway let's start with the bad news.** The guys who run the show in Washington are never going to change. I realize that in this book I have been an advocate for change. But here are the reasons they won't change. It doesn't matter if they are conservatives or if they are liberals. They spend millions of dollars to get a job that supposedly pays only few hundred thousand bucks a year. You don't have to be Fellini to know that's a bad trade. Therefore we know the following. 1) They have flawed decision making processes. 2) If they have intentions of making more than a few hundred K a year (and most of them do) what conclusions can we draw? Their moral compasses are spinning like a three year old on a lubed "sit in spin." 3) There is a reason that they have the nick name "fat cats." This has not changed since the time of King George in England. ***Hey Buck rent these two Frank Capra flicks and tell me if they apply today.*** "Mr. Smith Goes to Washington" made in 1939 and "Meet John Doe" made in 1941. Examine the underlying messages of both of those movies and see if they are not just as relevant today. *Gee Pat politicians don't seem to know the basics of the Four Amps. You have an obsession with Capra films. You have referred to three of them in this book.* ***Stay with me Bucky the good news is coming.***

Ok Buck here is the good news. The federal government is made up of three branches including the bicameral legislature. *Come on Pat your confusing me to the point that I have a head ache and I am nauseous.* The founding fathers understood political human nature. They painfully set up this system so the guys described above could not go totally off the reservation. They were smart enough to know that the power seeking political animal does not change from generation to generation. It was true then and it is true now. Who were these founding fathers? They were rebels, entrepreneurs and some of the best thinkers in our history. They were decedents of brave people who left their ancestral homes. These people came from structured societies where they could not elevate themselves beyond the social economic positions of birth. What our forefathers did was create a blue print for a free society and it has worked. They gave us the system in which most citizens can aspire to whatever they want to be including serving in government. The system of checks and balances is designed so no individual office holder can act unilaterally. To the point of your confusion **Buck, the forefathers created a system so no one branch**

could control the total decision making process of our government.

One critical part of our freedom is that we live in a capitalistic society. (Remember our fore fathers were entrepreneurs). *Huh Pat I am so confused.* **Ok Buck I will be blunt the system is set up that the government can only muck things up to a point and we have to function in that given reality.** In other words the opportunity to work for our advancement is at the root of our freedom. Unfortunately at present we face critical political and economic challenges. But as long as we are free we can chart our own destiny one person at a time. For example the late seventies was also a period of great economic challenges. Interest rates were at double digits causing great difficulties throughout the economy. Did people make money in seventies? Yes. Here is the deal. There is never going to be total employment, a perfect economy, world peace or a totally clean environment (Sorry Al). We are human beings after all. But in the United States we are free to build, free to grow, and to free to add-value. Even with all of our challenges we still have stronger opportunities than any other country in the world. So if we stay true to our mission and stick to the core principles of the Four Amps, it really shouldn't matter what happens in Washington? Self-reliance flourishes in a capitalistic society. Sorry Stalin you tried it the other way and failed and now you want to be like us. *I get it now. We can succeed in spite of the imperfections of this still great free society.* **Buck I am starting to see what Mildred sees in you.** The Four Amps prove that we can overcome even the most powerful external factors. Counted or not I can succeed. If interest rates are high I can adjust; if taxes increase I can work harder; if energy is scarce I can consider alternatives. I can be a one man conglomerate and drive myself to new heights of success. *Wow Pat, I think I get your point.* Those kids back in the forties who landed on beaches and who jumped out of planes came home and continued to build a dynamic nation. After preserving our freedom in their youth they came back and built a strong economy. They didn't have Four Amps but as a generation they had stones big enough to power Manhattan on a hot August day. All things considered I still feel blessed to be a citizen of this great country.

Please understand that it was not my goal to politicize this book. However it is critical to understand the decay of our self-reliance caused by the growing dependence of Americans on their government. Due to my fascination with the news it is apparent to me that as a country we have developed into a society of entitlement. America used to be the place where self-reliance flourished. Have you ever noticed how hard immigrants have always worked when they come to our country? *Oh Mildred I can't take it. I think he is going to go off on Immigration reform rant.* **Relax Bucky that's not where I am going.** Immigrants work hard because they appreciate the opportunities available to them. These opportunities are advantages they did not have in their countries of origin. Many of them of them had to fight hard get here. We are born with these opportunities and we take them for granted. We have relaxed into a sense of self-imposed superiority and it hurts us. We all need a Four Amp shot in the arm. In the eighties our manufacturing was dealt a severe blow when foreign competition almost destroyed our auto industry. Then the majority of our manufacturing jobs left because someone on the other side of the globe was doing the work better and cheaper. Now we cannot even answer the phone for our own products. India does it. Now we realize that an incredible education system that was built by our grandparents and parents trails behind other nations in key areas like math and science. We need to get to the root of the problems in education and solve them quickly. The "not counted" have a big opportunity. We can assume positions of independent leadership and set a new example of creating and building through self-reliance. Let the rest of the country see the success of the Four Amp revolt in the "not counted" population.

Earlier we made mention of our parents' generation and their response when called to defend our freedom. Now let's look at our generation. We were the beneficiaries of the post-World War II boom in America. We have seen more technological advancements in our lives than any other generation in history. We were the peace, love and Mother Nature generation. Or was that just a good excuse to get high and have indiscriminate sex? Our generation built careers and lived the American dream. Owning one car and living in mom and dad's track house in the suburbs were not good enough for us. We sported two imported SUV's in the driveway of a home with square footage far beyond our needs. In our generation both parents worked so they could afford the grand vacation. This meant that children were dropped off at day care early in the morning and retrieved in time for dinner. Most of our generation's children seem to have become acquisitions like the SUVs and the large homes. The peace love and Mother Nature generation transformed itself into the conspicuous consumption generation. We had an appetite for debt and used our homes like credit cards. We were not there to nurture our children. Family time was reduced to having meals on the run, videos in the SUV and an impossible schedule of individual outside activities. Family life in our generation bears little resemblance to the family life of the World War II generation. Most of our parents protected the mortgage on the family home as if it were sacred. Most mothers stayed home to raise their children. Our children have been raised in day care centers, by television and in front of computer screens. We are a disenfranchised country. ***Buck, close your mouth and quit drooling this comes back to Four Amps.***

There was a time when neighbors talked to each other. Now we communicate with made up personas on the internet. Neighbors are strangers. There was a time when fellow commuters casually talked to each other while traveling to work. Now we listen to music, watch videos or work on our laptops rather than interacting with the person next to us. Our parent's generation was one of family, community and country, whereas our generation is one of isolated individuals. Is it no wonder that our actions and values are reflected in the leadership of our nation? Therein lays the problem in the soul of the nation. At one time our national soul is what separated us from the rest of the world. The American soul that existed when Pearl Harbor was attacked tens of thousands of seventeen and eighteen year old Americans responded to that aggression and committed to service. They left family, academic endeavors, artistic endeavors, athletic endeavors, girlfriends/boyfriends and jobs. They put their personal futures on hold to secure a free future for their country.

The national infrastructure has been neglected because of special interest groups, greed and just plain mismanagement. As a nation we produce more food than any other country in the world. Yet we have citizens going hungry including young children and the elderly. Our government pays for studies as ridiculous as the observation of a shrimp on a tread mill. Instead of watching the shrimp on the treadmill, why don't we put it in some kid's stomach? *But I like my shrimp fried;* not now **Bucky, this is critical stuff and fried shrimp contains too much cholesterol anyway.** We have the best medical system in the world yet it isn't accessible to many. A sixteen hundred page document does not seem to be the answer. As you know by now I was a senior manager and senior managers crave problem solving. I won't bore you with my solutions but in the areas of national hunger and medical care I have spent time asking myself what I would do to solve those issues given the opportunity? As I see it too many middlemen and too much greed are the common denominators preventing solutions to the problems.

Our sewers, bridges, and highways are crumbling. Our schools are falling behind the rest of the world. Our environment is taking a beating. We cannot afford to fix any of these problems because the country is laden with debt on the federal and state levels of government. We keep borrowing money as a nation with no true investment returns from the proceeds of the loans. Our country is like the person who borrows from one credit card to pay another credit card. Eventually this person runs out of credit cards. This is the "body" of the country at the present time. As you can see we lack in our national body in the same way we are lacking in our national soul.

As we discussed earlier the national mind is mired with the antics of Washington. Lobbyists, special interest groups and political action committees have been robbing the national mind for years. Our government does not have a blue print for making long term decisions. Without this blue print in place the government is forced to react in haste to every crisis. This brings me back to my point of borrowing money as a short term solution which only creates deeper long term problems. In addition our foreign lenders can at any time sell-off our loans which would cause an even more devastating impact on our economy. The truly intellectual Americans stay miles away from the political circus. Political reform is sometimes a method to skirt existing laws. Now you can see that the national mind, the national body and the national soul are in need of repair.

How does this situation get reversed? One person at a time in the same way would be soldiers lined up at induction centers after the Pearl Harbor attack. We can make an impact on our national problems one American at a time. In working towards our individual goals we can contribute to the common goal by using our personal faculties to the best of our abilities. Think back to the example of the brave "Apollo Thirteen" astronauts. Use your individual Four Amps and then help your neighbor to find his/her Four Amps. When the pilgrims landed on Plymouth Rock it is doubtful that they went in separate directions. They worked together for the common goal. Our nation is strong, rich, smart and resourceful. We weaken ourselves by dividing into factions and not helping each other. This sounds simple and utopian. But is the present situation preferable? It is time to help ourselves and our neighbors pursue the Four Amps.

The dichotomy of this book is that the Four Amps is a call to individual action which needs to work within a community. We have just read about how as a society we have become disenfranchised with our fellow Americans. Whether one uses his/her network or creates a mass marketing campaign to develop opportunities he/she will have to bring in the outside community. Do not only view the community as a potential customer but view it as a resource that must also be replenished. Yes we must take from our community but we must also remember to give back to our community. As we rebuild ourselves using the Four Amps we must also make the effort to assist our neighbors. The better you do the better your neighbor does and the country does.

CHAPTER 8

Wired

*A man's true estate of power and
riches is to be in himself; not in his
dwelling or position or external
relations, but in his own essential
character.*

Henry Ward Beecher

In this book we have discussed how we can modify or improve ourselves by making significant changes in our behavior. Change is slow. It can be retarded by shocks to our internal or external worlds. We have to be willing to stay the course. Setbacks can test one's will or even push us back to nonproductive lifestyles. If we fail in one area but are successful in another area we should still see improvement. Human beings differ from one and other. Individuality demands different degrees of change to succeed. So prayer might be replaced by meditation. Or if you have no outdoor garden to plant a rose bush, cultivate an indoor plant instead. This book is not gospel. It is designed to get you to continually think of positive actions needed to achieve a new form of success. It helps provide inner peace as you manage the challenges in a new quickly changing world.

A sense of calm confidence will begin to support your daily tasks. You will start to smile. And you may be surprised when other people gravitate towards you. When an athlete or an artist nears his/her peak, performing at an incredible level, they say they are in the "zone." I now live in the "zone" from the minute I wake up in the morning until I go to bed at night. *Mildred I think Pat wants me to learn how to dribble a basketball as if I am not sore enough from the yoga.* **Relax Bucky. I only want you to join me in the "zone."** Since I have made these changes many of my business colleagues have asked me "what's with you?" My answer to that question is that I'm together. I keep hearing "I want what you have." To think I used to look at these people with envy because they had a job, a boss and an office and now they want what I have. What a contrast to the bummed out chubby guy discussed in the first chapter. Now days

I smile at these people and say I control my own destiny and I love it. I have Four Amps. I am fifty six years old. I don't know where next semesters tuition is coming from. But my new empowerment gives me total confidence and peace of mind. With these new tools I know the tuition will get paid. My life will continue to improve with this incredible sense of calm. I sincerely hope others have the same experience.

I have lived with the Four Amps for some time now and I can report a significant reduction in stress, in fatigue and in idol fear. The increase in energy continues. The feeling of being extremely fit is a major driving force in my continued positive results. It feels just plain good. I walk with more confidence and I take more pride in my appearance. A dear colleague and a brother in the "not counted" ranks has known me for a few years. A year ago he observed me walking through the Atlanta airport with extreme difficulty and pain. I had to stop about every twenty feet due to an arterial condition in my legs. The other day we had a meeting. When we left and walked up hill on Michigan Avenue, he stopped looked at me. He said "I cannot believe what I am seeing and how well you are walking." His advice was "brother keep it up." My entire approach to health, fitness and diet is now a way of life. My cholesterol is at an all-time low. My blood pressure and pulse readings are better than they have been in decades. Instead of looking at life's challenges as a burden I am determined to have a long, healthy and prosperous life. I am a rain maker without a cloud in the sky.

My mind is significantly clearer now. I can focus and develop a strategic plan that I know I can deploy. In the midst of presentations or meetings my mind does not drift and I don't pressure myself for an immediate successful outcome. Instead I focus on the merit of the project at hand and the impact on the client. I am patient with my negotiations. I am succeeding due to my altered mental state that is programmed me to win Guess what? I found this year's tuition before I finished writing this book. This @#$%$#@ works! I am a one man office who manipulates documents on the computer and prepares what's needed for a professional presentation. I am my only office resource. I am relaxed and I carry myself as if I had the world in the palm of my hand. I have built in my mind mechanisms similar to firewalls. These mechanisms do not allow unrelated events or thoughts to distract me from the task at hand. I keep my mind in a positive mode. And those around me are observing my positive results. My mind no longer creates imaginary enemies akin to Quixote's windmills. My family sees my old self. I now look at adversity and challenges as new opportunities. I am empowered!

Nowhere on my birth certificate is it written that I must be employed by anyone to work or succeed in my life. My soul is peaceful. I do not worry about the future and I have total faith in myself and the people around me. I have joy in my life again. My outlook and all it has to offer has gone from despair to hope. Relationships with those near and dear to me improve daily. Seemingly negative external events no longer make me feel inadequate. I can take straw and spin it into gold. I can provide for my family by using the resources of my mind, of my body and of my soul. Honesty and openness make up the foundation of my inner peace. The occasional solitude of my professional life is a luxury not the self-imposed sentence I thought it was. Never again will I drop to my knees to ask God why certain things happen. Now I thank God for the tools and opportunities He has given to me.

You might be thinking to yourself I feel fit, my mind is razor sharp and I am spiritually in a good place but I still need to pay the bills. How do you monetize your new improved state? Examine your historical talents, past contacts and market those skills. Do not be afraid to put yourself out in the public eye. It has risk but it also has great rewards. The following examples are suggestions for managers. But for those of you in non-management jobs these ideas also apply to your individual skill sets. If you were a CFO (chief financial officer) and you had a talent for forensic accounting and identifying waste and fraud market yourself as such. Contact accounting and law firms and let them know of your availability. If you are a marketing specialist and have a good quantifiable track record start to identify companies that might be struggling and need a fresh approach. If you are a logistic expert offer your services to young growing companies. If manufacturing efficiencies are your forte avail your services to every manufacturing entity in your area. You are not looking for a full time position you are offering your services to augment their organizations. Due to economic conditions and pending legislation companies are more prone than ever to hiring part-time consultants rather than full time employees. Unfortunately many factors in this country are forcing the creation of more part time affiliations than full time employments. Maximize this opportunity and present your skills to position yourself with three or four clients which will hedge your cash flow against negative economic shifts.

Align your new specialty consulting organization with others who are "not counted" but are marketing different areas of expertise. If you are the above mentioned CFO and you know an independent consultant who specializes in marketing or business intelligence create bilateral agreements where you can cross market each other and subcontract each other's services. This approach gives you and your associates more to offer the client once you are in the door. While you are working on a project for one hundred and fifty dollars hour you have simultaneously referred a consultant to another one of your clients for a different discipline. This referral will result in an override for you. You both win. The consultant you have an agreement with is making money he/she normally would not have and your hourly return is increased. I have implemented this agreement with my partners from phantom consulting. We possess the Four Amps but we must also be financial mercenaries. Survival is a war that can be won with a fit body, sharp mind and clear soul. Mercenary does not have a negative connotation; it drills home the "for hire" element of our new lives. Your mind, contacts, experience and education have significant value now let us all unite and take our Four Amps and sell that value!

The Four Amps methodology is not rocket science. No pun intended. There is very little in this book you did not already know. Loss of income coupled with the fear of the inability to provide for those near and dear to you clouded your attitude thus hampering your abilities. The Four Amps approach is a common sense and decent process to help manage the challenges of contemporary life. Is it not practical to keep our physical being as healthy and as well groomed as possible? Is it not prudent to examine how we make decisions? Is it not internally gratifying to view life with a positive spirituality? Hopefully this book has helped you answer these three questions. A person who is driven by a strong moral compass, a fit body and a keen mind will achieve success. Sharing your new experiences with others compounds the returns on your efforts.

Do not be shy with your gifts and talents. Help others in need to achieve the Four Amps.

The creation of the Four Amp methodology made me realize many things. I have taken my freedoms and American blessings for granted. We read earlier how many immigrants arrived here and worked feverishly in this land of opportunity. I have to admit that I was guilty of assuming that all my freedoms were acquired without a price. The more I thought about my freedoms no matter how large or small they are the result of hundreds of thousands of Americans self-sacrificing their lives and limbs. The realization of these unselfish sacrifices makes my recollection of chapter one embarrassing. We have so much to be grateful for and should exhaust every opportunity to make ourselves and country better. It has been said many times in this book that the true gift we have received is to live in a free and capitalistic society. Capitalism is the engine that exalts the beauty of freedom. Individual capitalism is capitalism in its purest form. Our forefathers did not work for major conglomerates, they worked for themselves. Fight for your freedoms and expand your business opportunity's using the Four Amps. You are free to be your own boss.

In my professional life I have had the privilege of stewarding and therefore reversing the directions of two companies. Turning companies around is my true professional passion. I may not ever get a similar opportunity again. I am at peace with that. Both companies were in disparate industries from the industry where I received my formal training. I took the basic business tenants of the investment industry and brought them to the education and technology industries and it worked. In this book we traveled a journey analogous to the journeys I took with those two companies. We accomplished the turn-around of the self. We reviewed, modified and improved every department in our internal complex organization. For me it has been the most rewarding turn around in my professional experience. Now it is your time to utilize your mind, your body, your soul, your instincts, your contacts and all your resources to complete your turn-around. My wish for you is peace, fitness and a strong mind. Now it is time to meet your new boss. You!

I have Four Amps and I count, I count on myself. You can count on yourself as well.

Good bye Bucky and Mildred have a "Wonderful Life."

Bibliography

Print Materials:
Books

Antoninus, Marcus Aurelius
    Thoughts on Success. Chicago: J. Triumph Books, 1995.

Barton, Bruce
    Thoughts on Success. Chicago: J. Triumph Books, 1995.

Beecher, Bruce
    Thoughts on Success. Chicago: J. Triumph Books, 1995.

Emerson, Ralph Waldo
    Thoughts on Success. Chicago: J. Triumph Books, 1995.

Shek, Chiang Kai
    Thoughts on Success. Chicago: J. Triumph Books, 1995.

West, Lois Jolyon
    Thoughts on Success. Chicago: J. Triumph Books, 1995.

Periodicals

Alfred E. Neuman, Mad Magazine, EC Comics

Films

Mr. Smith Goes to Washington Screenplay by Sidney Buchman, Prod. Frank Capra. Perf. James Stewart and Jean Arthur. Columbia, 1939. Film

Meet John Doe Screenplay Robert Riskin, Prod. Frank Capra. Perf. Gary Cooper and Barbara Stanwyck. Warner Brothers, 1941. Film

It's a Wonderful Life Screenplay by Frances Goodrich, Albert Haskett, Jo Swerling and frank Capra. Prod. Frank Capra. Perf. James Stewart and Donna Reed. RKO Radio Pictures, 1946. Film

Apollo Thirteen Screenplay by William Broyles Jr. and Al Reinart. Perf. Tom Hanks and Gary Sinise. Universal Pictures. 1995. Film.

Music

"Launch" *Apollo Thirteen,* James Horner, n.d. CD.

For further information about the
topic and author please go to,

Fouramps.com or Notcounted.com

About the Author

Pat is a lifelong Chicagoan. He began his professional career in 1979 as a runner on the Chicago Board Options Exchange. Then he became a retail stock broker for several of Wall Street's largest and most prestigious firms. After sixteen years as a stockbroker he made the decision to pursue his MBA in management. Pat graduated from The University of Notre Dame, Mendoza College of Business in 1996. He then joined the university as an employee in the College of Business focusing on executive education. The next job assignment was as the director of the university's for profit media company. While at the media company, Pat demonstrated the ability to reverse the fortunes of an ailing operation. He left the university to accept a position as president of a technology company owned by one of the university's trustees who was also the founder one of Wall Street's most prestigious leverage buyout/private equity firms. After four success-ful years in that position, Pat decided to return home to Chicago. Since returning home em-ployment has been sporadic and Pat has had to constantly reinvent himself as a business consultant. In the past seven years Pat has felt the trials and tribulations as a not counted member of the labor participation rate. The peaks and valleys of the past seven years in-spired Pat to write this book with the hope of helping others who face the same challenges.